Revising
Prose

SCRIBNER ENGLISH SERIES

Revising Prose

Richard A. Lanham
University of California, Los Angeles

Charles Scribner's Sons

New York

Copyright © 1979 Richard A. Lanham

Library of Congress Cataloging in Publication Data

Lanham, Richard A.
Revising prose.

1. English language — Style.   I. Title.
PE1421.L297   808'.042   78-10446
ISBN 0-684-15987-2

This book published simultaneously
in the United States of America
and in Canada —
Copyright under the Berne Convention

Excerpt from "Bridge Over Troubled Water"
© 1969 Paul Simon. Used by permission.

    5 7 9 11 13 15 17 19   v/p   20 18 16 14 12 10 8 6 4

Printed in the United States of America

CONTENTS

PREFACE   vii

CHAPTER ONE

Who's Kicking Who?   1

CHAPTER TWO

Sentences and Shopping Bags   9

CHAPTER THREE

Sentence Length, Rhythm, and Sound   25

CHAPTER FOUR

Voice and Sight Feedback   50

CHAPTER FIVE

The Official Style   56

CHAPTER SIX

The School Style   80

CHAPTER SEVEN

Why Bother?   103

APPENDIX: TERMS   117

PREFACE

The more student papers I read, the more I think that America's current epidemic verbal ineptitude comes on two levels, rudimentary and stylistic. The rudimentary level is caused by a failure to teach simple functional literacy. Students on this level make mistakes from ignorance. They don't know the rules. On the stylistic level, though, something different happens. You are not so much making "writing errors" as trying, usually with indifferent success, to imitate a predominant style, one you see all around you. This style, which let's call "The Official Style," you'll find, too, in your textbooks and in the academic bureaucracy's official pronouncements. Naturally enough, you come to think that's what is expected of you and try to imitate it.

Revising Prose addresses this second, stylistic level of the verbal epidemic. It is concerned not with inspiration or argumentation but with stylistic revision. Maybe *translation* would be a better word — translating The Official Style into plain English. *Revising Prose* tries to make you self-conscious about what The Official Style is, what it means to write it, and how it can — and usually should — be translated into plain English. The Official Style comes in several dialects, bureaucratic, social-scientific, computer-engineering-military, but all exhibit the same basic attributes. They all build on the same central imbalance, a dominance of nouns and an atrophy of verbs, the triumph of stasis over action. This basic imbalance is easy to cure — if you want to cure it.

But when *do* you want to cure it? Students today often feel — sometimes with justification — that they will be penalized for writing plain English. In the academic bureaucracy, writing plain English seems like walking down the hall with nothing on. Such public places demand protective coloration. Furthermore, if you are going to write in The Official Style, how do you make sure you are writing a good and not a bad one? And if The Official Style is, all said and done, a bad prose style — and it is — what, then, can "good" and "bad" mean when applied to prose?

Revising Prose starts out by teaching revision. When you've learned how to do that, we'll reflect on what such revision is likely to do for you — and to you — in the bureaucratic world of the future. We ought then to be able to see what "good" and "bad" mean for prose, and what you are really doing when you revise.

People often argue that writing cannot be taught, and if they mean that inspiration cannot be commanded nor laziness banished, then of course they are right. But stylistic analysis — revision — is something else, a method, not a mystical rite. How we compose — pray for the muse, marshall our thoughts, find the willpower to glue backside to chair — these may be idiosyncratic, but revision belongs to the public domain. Anyone can learn it.

I've called my basic procedure for revision a Paramedic Method because it provides emergency therapy, a first-aid kit, not the art of medicine. The only real solution to America's literacy crisis is a mature and reflective training in verbal self-awareness. Once you have this, you'll see and correct ordinary mistakes almost in passing. If you don't have it, no amount of rule memorization will bring good prose. For prose style, like the rest of human experience, is too various to be adequately described by rules. We don't write by rule but by imitation — as you've no doubt found when you've tried your hand at The Official Style.

But you can't stop the world to get off and take a course in prose style. The paper is due next week. And so *Revising Prose*. It is intended to be a self-teaching text to accompany courses that require papers. Like paramedicine in underdeveloped countries, it does not attempt to teach a full body of knowledge but only to diagnose and cure existing disease. No one argues that the paramedic is equal to the doctor but only that he may be equal to the disease.

Since my classroom students no longer seem to know the basic terms of grammar, I've listed them in an Appendix. The prose examples used — the "Jim kicks Bill" paradigm excepted — all come from student papers or from writing in what, with some exaggeration, is called "the real world."

R. A. L.
Los Angeles, May, 1978

ACKNOWLEDGMENTS

I must thank my colleagues Carol Hartzog,
Joyce Peterson and Edward Condren for reading
drafts of *Revising Prose* and trying it out
in action. My greatest debt, however, is obvious —
to the UCLA students who not only provided
the examples but stimulated the frenzied-despair-
at-yet-another-repetition-of-the-same-advice
which causes textbooks (or at least this
textbook) to be born.

Revising
Prose

CHAPTER ONE

Who's Kicking Who?

No student these days feels comfortable writing simply "Jim kicks Bill." The system seems to require something like "One can easily see that a kicking situation is taking place between Bill and Jim." Or, "This is the kind of situation in which Jim is a kicker and Bill is a kickee." Jim cannot enjoy kicking Bill; no, for school use, it must be "Kicking Bill is an activity hugely enjoyed by Jim." Absurdly contrived examples? Here are some real ones:

> This sentence is in need of an active verb.

> There is a great deal of feeling and involvement in his description.

> Another noticeable feature of the passage is the use of nouns, not only in reference to the name of things present, but in achieving a more forceful description of the scene.

See what they have in common? They are like our Bill and Jim examples, assembled from strings of prepositional phrases glued together by that all-purpose epoxy "is." In each case the sentence's verbal force has been shunted into a noun and for a verb we make do with "is," the neutral copulative, the weakest verb in the language. Such sentences project no life, no vigor. They just "are."

And the "is" generates those strings of prepositional phrases fore and aft. It's so easy to fix. Look for the real action. Ask yourself, who's kicking who? (Yes, I know, it should be *whom,* but doesn't it sound stilted?)

In "This sentence is in need of an active verb," the action obviously lies in "need." And so, "This sentence needs an active verb." The needless prepositional phrase "in need of," simply disappears once we see who's kicking who. The sentence, animated by a real verb, comes alive, and in six words instead of nine. (If you've not paid attention to your own writing before, think of a lard factor [LF] of ⅓ to ½ as normal and don't stop revising until you've removed it).

In "There is a great deal of feeling and involvement in his description," where is the action? In "description" obviously. And so, "He describes the scene feelingly." Out go the "of" and "in" prepositional phrases. We've five words instead of twelve, even though I've added two ("The scene") as a direct object for "describes." And notice how the rhythm improves? The original galumphs, every cadence about the same length:

There is / a great deal / of feeling / and involvement / in his description. /

The "is"-plus-prepositional-phrase pattern aborts any possible shape or rhythm. Now for the third example.

"Another notable feature of the passage is the use of nouns" — stop right there. Notice how long this sentence takes to get going? Again, who's kicking who? The "passage" is "using" nouns. When you omit the opening tautology — you have proved that the passage is notable by noting it — it reads "The passage uses nouns." We've eliminated two prepositional phrases and gotten the sentence off to a snappier start. Now we get rid of three more by locating the action — in "naming." So, "The passage uses nouns not only to name things present . . .". Since "but in achieving a more forceful description of the scene" obviously wants to say "but to describe the scene more forcefully," two more prepositional phrases bite the dust. And the parallelism of "to name" and "to describe" now comes clear since they can get closer together.

So: "The passage uses nouns not only to name things present but to describe the scene more forcefully." (Ignore, for the time being, that "more forcefully" is an indefinite comparative — more forcefully than what?) Read the revision and the original aloud several times. Notice how that da-da-dum monotony has vanished? Along with seven prepositional phrases. And we're going with a lard factor of 45% (found by dividing the difference between the number of words in the original and the revision by the number of words in the original — in this case, $31 - 17 = 14 \div 30 = .45$). The sentence puts its action into its verbs.

The drill for this problem stands clear. Circle every form of "to be" ("is," "was," "will be," "seems to be") and every prepositional phrase. Then find out who's kicking who and start rebuilding the sentence with that action. Two prepositional phrases in a row turn on the warning light, three make a problem, and four invite disaster. With a little practice, sentences like "The mood Dickens paints is a bleak one" will turn into "Dickens paints a bleak mood" (LF 38%) almost before you've written them. And you'll just not commit the Normative Undergraduate Sentence, the pure formula:

> Central to our understanding of the character of Lucrece in William Shakespeare's *The Rape of Lucrece* is the long passage toward the end of the poem devoted to a painting of the fall of Troy.

A diagram may help:

Central to our understanding
    of the character
    of Lucrece
    in William Shakespeare's *The Rape of Lucrece*
is the long passage
    towards the end
    of the poem devoted
    to a painting
    of the fall
    of Troy.

Four prepositional phrases in a row glued to five preposi-tional phrases in a row by nothing but an epoxy "is" and hope. The catalogue-like monotony shines through the diagram. And how long it takes to get going! The rocket fires, fizzles through "to" da-da-dum, "of" and "in," and then hits "is" and falls back dead onto the launching pad. How to fix it?

Again, where's the action? Here, buried not in a word but in a phrase, "central to our understanding." We need a verb — "reveals," "illuminates," "focuses," "explains," "analyzes." Try "illuminates": the actor, the Troy paint-ing, illuminates Lucrece's character. "The Troy painting, described near the poem's end, illuminates Lucrece's character." Eleven words instead of thirty-five — LF 68%.

The Normative Undergraduate Sentence does not, of course, always come from undergraduates. Look at these "of" strings from a linguist, a literary critic, and a popular gourmet.

It is the totality *of* the interrelation *of* the various com-ponents *of* language and the other communication systems which is the basis for referential memory.

These examples *of* unusual appropriateness *of* the sense *of* adequacy to the situation suggest the primary signification *of* rhyme in the usual run *of* lyric poetry.

> Frozen breads and frozen pastry completed the pro-
> cess *of* depriving the American woman *of* the pleasure
> *of* boasting *of* her baking.

The "of" strings are the worst of all. They look like a child
pulling a gob of bubble gum out into a long string. When
you try to revise them, you can feel how fatally easy the "is
and of" formulation can be for expository prose. And
how fatally confusing, too, since to find an active, transitive verb for "is" means, often, adding a specificity the
writer has not provided. So, in the first example, what
does "is the basis for" really mean? And does the writer
mean that language's components interact with "other
communication systems," or is he talking about "components" of "other communication systems" as well? The
"of" phrases refer back to those going before in so general
a way that you can't keep straight what really modifies
what. So revision here is partly a guess.

> Referential meaning emerges when the components
> of language interact with other communication sys-
> tems.

Or the sentence might mean

> Referential meaning emerges when the components
> of language interact with the components of other
> communication systems.

Do you see the writer's problem? He has tried to be
more specific than he needs to be, to build his sentence on
a noun ("totality") which demands a string of "of's" to
qualify it. Ask where the action is, build the sentence on a
verb, and the "totality" follows as an implication. Noun-
centeredness like this generates most of our present-day
prose sludge.

The second example, out of context, doesn't make

much sense. Perhaps "These examples, where adequacy to the situation seems unusually appropriate, suggest how rhyme usually works in lyric poetry." The third is easy to fix. Try it.

In asking who's kicking who, a couple of mechanical tricks come in handy. Besides getting rid of the "is's" and changing every passive voice ("is defended by") to an active voice ("defends"), you can squeeze the compound verbs hard, make every "are able to" into a "can," every "seems to succeed in creating" into "creates," every "cognize the fact that" (no, I didn't make it up) into "think," every "am hopeful that" into "hope," every "provides us with an example of" into "exemplify," every "seeks to reveal" into "shows," every "there is the inclusion of" into "includes."

And you can amputate those mindless introductory phrases, "The fact of the matter is that" and "The nature of the case is that." Start fast and then, as they say in the movies, "cut to the chase" as soon as you can. Instead of "the answer is in the negative," you'll find yourself saying "No."

We now have the beginnings of a Paramedic Method (PM):

1. Circle the prepositions.
2. Circle the "is" forms.
3. Ask "Who is kicking who?"
4. Put this "kicking" action in a simple (not compound) active verb.
5. Start fast — no mindless introductions.

Try out the PM on the following examples. The nonfat versions ought to be half as long and have some zip.

1. The many nouns help you to vividly see numerous things, but there is very little action.

2. I feel *Venus and Adonis* is a satire primarily because of the extreme nature of the mismatch of the two characters.

3. The poem is an allegory of the evolution of the role figures of medieval times to the self-conscious egotist of the Renaissance.

4. The central plot interest of Shakespeare's poem *Venus and Adonis,* Adonis's adamant rejection of Venus's unflagging courtship, is entirely contrary to Ovid's account of the story in *Metamorphoses* and to the original Greek myth.

5. One particularly enticing example of this aspect of water symbolism is the reference to Narcissus kissing himself in the brook.

6. The play is an allegorization of the conception and development of a new concept of justice delivered by the character Angelo and embodied in the character of the Duke.

7. Lost in the rewrite is the intrigue that the reader experienced when wondering what message the author was trying to convey by writing in such an odd fashion. What was gained in the normalized version was a smoother reading and a greater understanding of what was going on.

8. As the churchmen are officially viewed as bastions of virtue in society, the inference that we are expected to draw from this is that it is thus virtuous to squander one's fortune, a proposition logically arrived at but nonetheless false.

9. The techniques proposed here were obtained, in part, by adapting, for qualitative variables, some of the multiple-comparison ideas proposed earlier in the analysis of variance context. This adaptation for the analysis of qualitative variables was carried out in an earlier series of articles by the present author in which simultaneous confidence intervals and multiple test procedures were devel-

oped for the simultaneous analysis of a variety of questions pertaining to a given qualitative variable or to a given set of qualitative variables.

10. Dear Faculty Member,

A program is being developed for implementation in the spring of 1972 that will include the University in the decision-making process which affects all of our lives. Special Studies Workshops for Policy Proposal is a new curriculum whose intent it is to discover the needs of the decision-makers, the expertise of the faculty, and the interests of the students, and bring all three together in the workshops.

CHAPTER TWO

Sentences and Shopping Bags

None of the sentences you've just worked through has any shape. They just go on and on, as if they were emerging from a nonstop sausage machine. This shapelessness makes them unreadable: you cannot read them aloud with expressive emphasis. Try to. When language as spoken and heard has completely atrophied, the sentence becomes less a shaped unit of emphatic utterance than a shopping bag of words. Read your own prose aloud and with emphasis — or better still, have a friend read it to you. This rehearsal can often tell you more about the shape, rhythm, and emphasis of your sentences than any other single device. You might try, too, writing a single sentence on a sheet of blank paper. Forget your profound meaning for a minute and just look at the sentence's shape. Try to isolate the basic parts and trace their relationship to one another.

We'll lead off with a monster:

The fact that all selves are constituted by or in terms of the social process, and are individual reflections of it — or rather of this organized behavior pattern which it exhibits, and which they comprehend in their respective structures — is not in the least incompatible with or destructive of the fact that every individual self has its own peculiar individuality, its unique pattern; because each individual within that process, while it reflects in its organized structure the behavior patterns of that process as a whole, does so from its own particular and unique standpoint within that process, and thus reflects in its organized structure a different aspect or perspective of this whole social behavior pattern from that which is reflected in the organized structure of any other individual self within that process (just as every monad in the Leibnizian universe mirrors that universe from a different point of view, and thus mirrors a different aspect or perspective of that universe).

None of the usual definitions of a sentence really says much, but every sentence ought somehow to organize a pattern of thought, even if it does not always reduce that thought to bite-sized pieces. This shapeless hippo, however, has at heart only our getting lost. Notice how far it is from the first subject ("the fact that") to its verb ("is")? We forget the subject before we get to the verb. To bring some shape to this shopping bag, we'll have, for a start, to put a full stop after "pattern." "The fact that" translates, as always, into "that." And then we return to changing passive voice to active voice ("are constituted by" to "constitutes"), to eliminating prepositional phrases, to finding out where the action is (who is kicking who). And we must attack, too, the compulsive pattern of needless overspecification ("incompatible with, or destructive of"), the endemic curse of academic writing from the cradle to the grave. So: "That society (= "the social process") constitutes all selves and they reflect it . . .". So far so good. What of the two lines between — and — ? They simply restate, in new gobbledegook terminology, what has preceeded. Shred them. And "is not in the least incompatible with or destructive of the fact that" translates into English as "does not in the least destroy." "Every individual self has its own peculiar individuality, its own unique pattern" = "the unique self." We have translated the first half of this shopping bag back into English as:

> That society constitutes all selves and they reflect it, does not in the least destroy the unique self. (Eighteen words instead of sixty-five; LF 72%).

To finish shaping this sentence, we need only add a comma after "selves." Now read it aloud. Subject ("That society constitutes all selves") separated from its verb by only a short parenthetical addition ("and they reflect it") stays in our mind until we reach a direct object ("the unique self"), which falls into the naturally emphatic closing position. The voice ought to rise in pitch for the parenthetic "they reflect" and for "least" and "unique." The sentence shape underscores its meaning rather than burying it. The syntax permits, encourages, the voice to help. The prose has become readable. See if you can clean up the rest of the passage in the same way.

Looking for the natural shape of a sentence often suggests the quickest way to revision. Consider this example:

> I think that all I can usefully say on this point is that in the normal course of their professional activities social anthropologists are usually concerned with the third of these alternatives, while the other two levels are treated as raw data for analysis.

The action starts with "are usually concerned with." Beginning to build a shape means starting here. "Usually, social anthropologists concentrate on the third alternative. . . ." And now, do we really need the whole endless dead-rocket opening, from "I think" to "activities"? "In the normal course of their professional activities" = "usually," and the rest is guff. So: "Usually, social anthropologists concentrate on the third alternative and treat the other two as raw data" ("for analysis" being implied by "raw data"). A final polishing moves "usually" to the other side of "social anthropologists" so as to modify "concentrate" more immediately. The sentence then begins strongly, subject — short modifier — verb, and offers two other emphasis points, "third alternative" and "raw data." And shouldn't we subordinate the "treat" by turning it into a participle? The final revision would then read, "Social anthropologists usually concentrate on the third alternative, treating the other two as raw data." Read it aloud now and then go back to the original and compare (fifteen words instead of forty-five; LF 66%).

Prose, then, unlike beefsteak, does not become more choice when marbled with fat. Because fat in prose, as in our bodies, affects the shape more immediately than the meaning, a feeling for shape and emphasis constitutes our best weapon against wordiness. A few undergraduate instances will show how a shopping-bag sentence can be given some shape.

> A piece of prose may be considered sincere if, in some manner, it establishes its credibility to its audience. The degree of sincerity, however, is relative to the type of person reading it. A logical, scientific person would feel gratified if the author included the relationship of counterpoints to his message. To them this technique shows that the author considered opposing viewpoints while presenting his own; an analytical ideal for such an audience.

A typical piece of shapeless prose. Tedious. Lifeless. Just plain boring to read. The first sentence ought by its shape to underline the basic contrast of "sincere" with "credible." How about, "Prose will seem sincere if it seems credible"? The parallelism of "seems sincere" and "seems credible" works because the two parallel elements stand close together. Sparks can fly between them. The sentence gains some snap, a shape (eight words instead of nineteen; LF 58%). Now for the second sentence. It qualifies the first and should do so obviously. We need an adversative, "but": "But how sincere will depend on the type of reader." Or maybe just "on the reader," "type of" and "kind of" being usually expendable qualifiers. Now read the last two sentences aloud, and with feeling — *con amore.* Can't be done. Where, though, does your voice *want* to rise, what does it *want* to stress? Obviously "a logical scientific person" and "opposing viewpoints." What shape will model this? "A logical, scientific person" = "A scientist"; "would feel gratified" = "would welcome"; "if the other included the relationship of counterpoints to his message" = "would welcome a statement of alternative views." In the last sentence, "to them" refers back, impossibly enough, to a singular antecedent ("scientific person") and the rest is inane repetition. What follows after the semicolon represents dieselizing — the prose engine continuing to run after the key has been turned off. It indicates that a sense of shape means a feeling for strong closings as well as strong openings. As a revision, then: "A scientist would welcome a statement of alternative views." (nine words for forty; LF 78%). And for the whole passage:

> Prose will seem sincere if it seems credible. But how sincere will depend on the (type of) reader. A scientist would welcome a statement of alternative views.

We've solved a number of problems but we've created some too, first in the sequence of thought and, scarcely less obviously, in the rhythmic interrelation of the three sentences. The prose sounds choppy. It often happens in elephantiasis surgery like this and can't be helped. Don't worry. Concentrate on the shape of each sentence. If, as here, you end up with a string of sentences all the same length, this can be fixed later.

To articulate the sequence of thought, we need to join

the first two sentences and acknowledge the third as an example:

Prose will seem sincere if it seems cred . . .

Now the real problem emerges. What depends *directly* on the reader is credibility, not sincerity. The writer was trying to say: "Prose will seem sincere if it seems credible, but how credible will depend on who reads it." "Who reads it" finally gets around the awkward "type of" problem and leads directly to "A scientist." Now that we've gotten this straight, the last sentence follows naturally as an example of how credibility varies with the reader: "A scientist, for example, would welcome a statement of alternative views." And so again, original and revision:

ORIGINAL

A piece of prose may be considered sincere if, in some manner, it establishes its credibility to its audience. The degree of sincerity, however, is relative to the type of person reading it. A logical scientific person would feel gratified if the author included the relationship of counterpoints to his message. To them this technique shows that the author considered opposing viewpoints while presenting his own; an analytical ideal for such an audience.

REVISION

Prose will seem sincere if it seems credible, but how credible will depend on who reads it. A scientist, for example, would welcome a candid statement of alternative views.

I've inserted "candid" both because it clarifies the credibility issue we've just brought into focus and because the rhythm needs another beat or two here, a kind of adjectival rest before the stressed "statement of alternative views." This back pressure of rhythm on sense illustrates in little just what the whole passage does in large. Thought and style feed back on one another continually as you revise prose. Leaning on rhythm means leaning on thought, and vice versa. And the process never ends.

We've taken this passage about as far as it will go, but one problem still remains. The rhythm seems okay (try it, as always, by reading it aloud with emphasis and coloration), but both sentences run to about the same length. For this reason, the one which follows this passage ought to be either much longer or very short.

When prose is read aloud, sentence shape presents few problems. The voice can shape and punctuate as it goes along. But when the voice atrophies, the eye does not make the same demands with equal insistence, and the larger shaping rhythms that build through a paragraph tend to blur. A problem hard to see and hard to remedy. Consider this passage from a recent popular article by an American economist.

> A third advantage of the market as a means of social organization is its "devil-take-the-hindmost" approach to questions of individual equity. At first blush this is an outrageous statement worthy of the coldest heart among the nineteenth-century Benthamites. And obviously I have stated the point in a way more designed to catch the eye than to be precise.
>
> In any except a completely stagnant society, an efficient use of resources requires constant change. Consumer tastes, production technologies, locational advantages, and resource availabilities are always in flux. From the standpoint of static efficiency, the more completely and rapidly the economy shifts production to meet changes in tastes, resource availability or locational advantages, the greater the efficiency. From a dynamic standpoint, the greater the advances in technology and the faster they're adopted, the

greater the efficiency. While these changes on balance generate gains for society in the form of higher living standards, almost every one of them causes a loss of income to some firms and individuals, often temporary and for only a few, but sometimes long-lasting and for large numbers.

What do you notice? Well, that first sentence, for a start — an almost perfect Normative Undergraduate Sentence, though now from a high government official:

A third advantage
of the market
as a means
of social organization
is
its "devil-take-the-hindmost" approach
to questions
of individual equity.

Although the sentences do not run to an exact length, they are mostly long and mostly monotonous. No short sentences mean no large-scale emphasis, no climax and finality. The last sentence of paragraph two, though much shorter than any other, doesn't summarize anything. How to supply some shape? For a start, get the lard out of the first paragraph:

A third advantage of the market as a means of social organization rests in its "devil-take-the-hindmost" approach to individual equity. At first blush this seems outrageous statement worthy of the coldest heart. Benthamite And obviously I have stated the point

~~a way more designed~~ to catch the eye ~~than to be precise~~.

What has been done? I've made one assumption the writer did not, that the audience knows "Benthamite" means "nineteenth century." Otherwise, only fat has been removed. The rhythm has picked up a little. The first sentence now begins more quickly and it has a real verb (though "rests" may not be ideal — how about "remains" or "stands"?). Phrases like "questions of," "problems of," "factors of" are simply mindless fillers, bad habits like "like" and "you know" after every third word. An unqualified substantive, paradoxically, almost always comes across stronger. The changes in the second sentence all aim to increase the emphasis on "outrageous statement." In the third, I've tried to underscore the parallelism of "stated the point" and "catch the eye."

The original and revision to date:

ORIGINAL

A third advantage of the market as a means of social organization is its "devil-take-the-hindmost" approach to questions of individual equity. At first blush this is an outrageous statement worthy of the coldest heart among the nineteenth-century Benthamites. And obviously I have stated the point in a way more designed to catch the eye than to be precise.

REVISION

The market's third advantage as a social organization rests in its "devil-take-the-hindmost" approach to individual equity. This outrageous statement seems, at first blush, worthy of the coldest Benthamite heart. And obviously I have stated the point to catch the eye. (LF 33%)

Sentence lengths of 19–13–11 instead of 24–18–20. The result may still fall short of Keats, but at least a decreasing-length pattern has begun to form and the last sentence has a bit of zip. Sometimes little changes take you a long way:

~~In any~~ *E*xcept ^*in* a ~~completely~~ stagnant society, ~~an~~

efficient use of resources requires constant change.

Again, the adverbial intensifier ("completely") weakens instead of strengthens. And we want to get to "stagnant society" more quickly. Read the two versions aloud several times. Does the revision succeed in placing more stress on "constant change"? The same desire for end-stress now changes "are always in flux" to "always change" in the next sentence. And again in the following one:

~~From the~~ *For* ~~standpoint of~~ static efficiency, the more

~~completely and~~ rapidly the economy shifts production

to meet chang~~es~~*ing* ~~in~~ taste*s*^ resource*s*^ ~~availability~~, or

locational advantages the ~~greater the efficiency~~ *better*^. [And

couldn't we say "locations" rather than "locational

advantages"?]

Now we want to preserve the static/dynamic contrast he is developing—"for static efficiency/for dynamic efficiency":

For ~~From a~~ dynamic ~~standpoint~~, the *efficiency* ~~greater~~ *faster* the ~~advances~~

~~in technology and the faster they are adopted~~ *technological change*, the

~~greater the efficiency~~ *better*.

The two sentences still end with the same phrase, but since they connect more closely the prose no longer sounds like a list or catalogue.

The curse of academic writing, again, is spelling everything out. Academics prepare an assertion the way a cook prepares abalone, by beating it repeatedly with a hammer to make it tender. So in the previous sentence, and in the one which follows:

> While these changes ~~on balance~~ generate ~~gains for society in the form of~~ higher living standards, almost [*all*] ~~every one of them~~ ~~causes a loss of~~ [*decrease*] income, ~~to some firms and individuals,~~ often temporarily and for ~~only~~ a few, but sometimes [*permanently*] ~~long lasting~~ and for [*many*] ~~larger numbers~~.
>
> (LF 50%)

The sense may require "on balance," but the rest is pure lard. Again, the ending parallelism is stressed:

temporarily and for a few

permanently and for many.

Our revision to date, then, reads like this:

> The market's third advantage as a social organization rests in its "devil-take-the-hindmost" approach to individual equity. This outrageous statement seems, at first blush, worthy of the coldest Benthamite heart. And obviously I have stated the point to catch the eye.
>
> Except in a stagnant society, efficient use of resources requires constant change. For static efficiency, the more rapidly the economy shifts production to meet changing tastes, resources, or locations, the bet-

ter. For dynamic efficiency, the faster the technological change, the better. While these changes generate higher living standards, almost all decrease income, often temporarily and for a few, but sometimes
permanently and for many. (LF 42%)

Sentence length varies enough to stave off monotony and
to support, even if it does not specifically illuminate, the
argument. Something like a climactic structure has
emerged from the second paragraph. I didn't strive for
this. After you've squeezed out the lard, it emerges by itself.

Here is a final instance of how shape and voice interact. In the original version, the student has written a
prose that considers neither the eye nor the ear. You can
make sense of it, but it doesn't give you any help. Try
reading it aloud.

ORIGINAL

In William Shakespeare's *Measure for Measure,* the
behind-the-scenes activity of the Duke, visible to the
audience but invisible to the rest of the players,
directs the dramatic action; in a sense, the drama represents the thought process of the Duke. He retires
from public view and places Angelo in his office.
Since he is freed from the limitations of his official
public position, he can adopt a different viewpoint,
private and spiritual. Interacting with his citizens as
individuals, instead of a populace subject to one absolute law, he can exercise subjective judgment. As
would an executive of secular law, he orders men's
lives. He manipulates the characters of the play and
reorganizes the structure of their relationships. However, as a friar, he can do so as a personification of
general moral principles appearing to each person

uniquely. When the duke resumes his office, his new evaluation of justice is a synthesis of laxity and severity, a newly weighed balance of grace and punishment.

The revision, which the student has done using the Paramedic Method, creates a genuinely readable prose, prose that shapes its meaning rather than simply containing it.

REVISION

In *Measure for Measure,* the Duke's behind-the-scenes activity, visible only to the audience, shapes the other characters' fates. The Duke is freed from the limited perspective of his public role, and he adopts a friar's viewpoint, private and spiritual. Seeing his subjects as individuals, he can then judge them both justly and mercifully. When he resumes office, he applies a newly weighed balance of grace and punishment. His power is revitalized. (72 words instead of 174; LF 59%)

We can now add two more diagnostic procedures to our Paramedic Method:

1. Circle the prepositions.
2. Circle the "is" forms.
3. Ask, "Who is kicking who?"
4. Put this "kicking" action in a simple (not compound) active verb.
5. Start fast — no mindless introductions.
6. Write out the sentence on a blank sheet of paper and look at its shape.
7. Read the sentence aloud with emphasis and feeling.

Here are some shopping bags which, using the PM, you can revise into real sentences.

1. The surrealistic episode which uses nouns rather than verbs as its descriptive force imparts to the reader the feeling of stillness because it has no action words to put motion into the scene.

2. At the beginning of the passage the scene is set simply with the use of the word "London." Without the use of any other words to reveal the vantage point of the author we don't know if he is observing the objects he is writing down, whether he has just heard of them, or just what the situation is.

3. Probably the most insincere style attempts to make a reader feel so ignorant in his knowledge of the subject he is reading about that he blindly accepts what one author has to say.

4. Buchwald places two conditions on his readers in order for them to benefit from his articles. First, the reader should have some knowledge on the political scene to comprehend fully the points and ideas he attempts to develop.

5. Like a swarm of ants they seem to come endlessly to smother you as they go through their routine.

6. Edmund Burke's passage from *Reflections on the Revolution in France* employs a predicative stance in trying to get the point across to the reader or listener that when the French people embrace religion and altruism, and when they become conscious of the power they wield, only then will they nominate to public office representatives of virtue and wisdom.

7. The single outstanding similarity in comparing the poem with the myth consists of the almost identical arrangement of scenes and speeches of both Shakespeare's Venus and the Venus of the myth during their admonishments to their respective Adonis' about dangerous game.

8. Legislators in Sacramento and Washington have been polled and we have lists of both general and specific topics in which they have legislative interest. The workshops will gather data on as many facets as possible of any

problem and draw policy proposals from their data. The legislators have told us that they will use the results of the workshops in either constructing new legislation or amending and voting on existent legislation.

9. The first is a paper shortage that is already being felt throughout the publishing industry. The impact of this shortage is that it is not a short term problem but will be with us for some time to come and can seriously affect the number of books produced by the industry. There are a number of reasons why we are faced with a shortage at this time. Paper mills are eliminating from their production schedules uneconomical marginal papers and specialty papers, concentrating instead on the production of more profitable lines of paper.

10. There are two faculty committees which have been assigned the responsibility of reviewing and evaluating this Extended University program. The M.Arch.II Curriculum Committee has been instrumental in preparing this proposal and will continue to maintain its surveillance of this program as part of its responsibilities for overall evaluation and supervision of the M.Arch. II curriculum. The Grading and Evaluation Committee is responsible for conducting evaluations of all architecture and urban design courses, and for developing policies and procedures for student evaluation. Upon request, the reports of these two committees will be made available to the Graduate Council.

11. A Marshall Scholar, as the possessor of a keen intellect and a broad outlook, will be thought of as a person who would contribute to the aims which the late General Marshall had in mind when, on 5th June, 1947, at Cambridge, Massachusetts, he spoke of economic assistance for Europe, and said "An essential part of any successful action on the part of the United States is an understanding on the part of the people of America of the character of the problem and the remedies to be applied."

12. The title given to these few, too brief, remarks on

the scope and implications of a possible semiotic approach to the practice of the Arts is, with its false simplicity, *suspect,* like all titles of this double-entry type (art and revolution, civilization and technology, etc.) where two uncertainly defined terms are coordinated in the service of a demonstration, usually of an ideological nature. For this conjunction can, according to circumstances, denote union just as much as opposition (semiotics as allied to iconography or, conversely, as its opponent?), adjunction as much as exclusion (semiotics *and* iconography, semiotics *or* iconography), even dependence (iconography as the servant of semiotics, or conversely as its "blueprint," in the sense that, as for Saussure, linguistics was to be the "blueprint" of all semiology).

CHAPTER THREE

Sentence Length, Rhythm, and Sound

Take a piece of your prose and a red pencil and draw a slash after every sentence. Two or three pages ought to make a large enough sample. If the red marks occur at regular intervals, you have, as they used to say in the White House, a problem. You can chart the problem another way, if you like. Choose a standard length for one sentence and then do a bar-graph. If it looks like this,

dandy. If like this,

not so dandy. Obviously, no absolute quantitative standards exist for how much variety is good, how little bad, but the principle couldn't be easier. Vary your sentence lengths. Naturally enough, complex patterns will fall into long sentences and emphatic conclusions work well when short. But no rules prevail except to avoid monotony.

Here is a before-and-after piece of student prose that illustrates the problem perfectly:

BEFORE

Niccolo Machiavelli has been vilified for almost five centuries for suggesting a new paradigm for human behavior which is only now emerging in the literature of the behavioral sciences. / In his *Il Principe* of 1513 Machiavelli sets forth observations about social reality which are closer in sensibility to our present post-Darwinian perspective than to that of the intelligentsia of *cinquecento* Italy, steeped as they were in the Neo-Platonic notions of order, harmony, goodness, beauty, moral action, and divine Providence set forth so clearly in Baldassare Castiglione's *Il Cortegiano*. / Machiavelli, by pushing to its extreme the Castiglionean concept of the self-as-a-work-of-art, and by withdrawing the ethical considerations from the Renaissance's preoccupation with the disjunction of appearance and reality, posits a well-functioning social order which is in effect, a play written and directed by its prime role-player, the prince. / Like a modern sociologist, Machiavelli bases his behavioral theories on observed fact and like a true humanist, he draws these facts from the realms of contemporary and classical Italy: ". . . non ho trovato . . . cosa quale io abbi più cara o tanto esistimi quanto la cagnizione delle azioni degli uomini grandi, imparata da me con una lunga esperienza delle cose moderne e una continua lezione delle antique. . . ." / Above all else, Machiavelli's observations of these "uomini grandi" lead him to shun Castiglione's equation of the esthetic with the moral and to redefine "virtu" as "ingegno," that practical ability which enables a prince to cope with a world in which there are "tanti che non sono buoni" by learning to be "non buono, e usarlo e non l'usare secondo la necessità"; to appear to be "pietoso, fidele, umano, intero, religioso, ed essere; ma stare in modo . . . che, bisognando non essere, tu possa e sappi mutare el contrario." /

Any length so long as it is long! The passage includes, in fact, most of the problems the Paramedic Method tries to solve. The student's revision, which applies the PM, turns night into day.

AFTER

Machiavelli has long been vilified for suggesting a behavioral paradigm only now emerging in the behavioral sciences. / Though published in 1513, *Il Principe* describes a social reality closer to our post-Darwinian perspective than to *cinquecento* Neo-Platonism. / Like a modern sociologist, Machiavelli generalizes from observed fact. / And like a true humanist he studies both contemporary and Classical Italy: ". . . non ho trovato . . . cosa quale io abbi più cara o tanto esistimi quanto la cagnizione delle azioni degli uomini grandi, imparata da me con una lunga esperienza delle cose moderne e una continua lezione delle antique. . . ." / Observing these "uomini grandi," Machiavelli concludes that a prince must learn to be "non buono, e usarlo e non l'usare secondo la necessità." / He shuns the Neo-Platonic equation of "ingegno" and "virtu." / Political success requires duplicity. /

Sentence length varies here and the final sentence gains summary force because it is short. The passage takes on a larger shape, short and medium-length sentences grouped around a long central one that includes an extensive quotation. But obviously, the revision changes much else besides sentence length.

The elements of prose style — grammar, syntax, shape, rhythm, emphasis, level, usage, and so on — all work as dependent variables. Change one and, to some extent, you change the rest. Rhythm and sound seem, for most prose writers, the most dependent of all. They affect nothing and everything affects them. They do affect something, though. They affect us. Rhythm constitutes the most vital of prose's vital life-signs. Rhythmless, unemphatic prose always indicates that something has gone wrong. And Tin Ears, insensitivity to the sound of words, indicate that the hearing which registers rhythm has been turned off.

Tin Ears have become so common that often you can't tell mistakes from mindlessness. A flack for the army writes:

> Like any new departure in motivating men, the path to a Modern Volunteer Army is beset with perils and pitfalls but it also has potential for progress.

Is the alliteration of "*m*otivating *m*en," "*p*erils and *p*itfalls," "*p*otential for *p*rogress" intended or accidental? It works, at all events, obvious though it may be. The three central phrases of the sentence are spotlighted by an alliterated pair of words, and the last two pairs are put into almost visual contrast:

> perils and pitfalls
> potential for progress

And "motivating men" finds an alliterative echo in "Modern" while the *p* alliteration has a pre-echo in "path." All this seems to indicate premeditation and a heavy hand. But the writer obviously creates a specific shape and rhythm.

Not so in the following sentence:

> For the writer, the practice of bad writing is harmful, for it results in an inhibition of his responses to intellectual and imaginative stimuli.

Notice the "*in an in*hibition" sequence, forcing the reader to babble? And did the writer see the "harm*ful for*" doublet? Notice how it works against his purpose here? The punctuation encourages us to stop after "harmful" while the *ful–for* alliterative couplet wants us to rush on without a stop. And he has another mouthful-of-peanut-butter *n-m* cluster in "respo*n*ses to *in*tellectual and *im*agi*n*ative stimuli." I've deliberately chosen an example where this unspeakable cluster did *not* stand out, just to show how often one is there, nevertheless. Prose will always possess a spoken dimension so long as we continue to speak. If we ignore it, it will not go away; it will come back to plague us. How to fix this example? First, the standard drill. Circle the prepositions. Get rid of "is." Ask who is kicking who. Squeeze out the lard. Here is the original again:

> (For) the writer, the practice (of) bad writing (is) harmful, for it results (in) an inhibition (of) his responses (to) intellectual and imaginative stimuli.

The actor is "bad writing" and the action lies buried in "inhibition." So: "Bad writing inhibits a writer's intellect and imagination" (LF 66%). "The practice of" is one of those "the fact that" fillers. "Results in an inhibition of" is one of those "is"-plus-noun-plus-preposition substitutions for the simple verb "inhibits," like "stands in violation of" for "violates." "Harmful" is implied by "inhibits." "Responses to intellectual and imaginative stimuli," means simply "intellect and imagination." And so we have "Bad writing inhibits a writer's intellect and imagination." And, since our subject is Tin Ears, we notice right away that "mind" instead of "intellect" smooths out that *intellect* and *imagination* cluster of *m*'s, *n*'s, and *t*'s. "Bad writing inhibits a writer's mind and imagination." We've also substituted a single-syllable word for a three-syllable word, and this helps out in a sentence already overloaded with two- and three-syllable words. Notice how they monotonize the rhythm?

What has happened here? We've revised the sentence with our do-it-yourself PM and the rhythmless morass has taken care of itself. Interdependent variables, again. Find out who is kicking who, and the problems that fan out from this central misapprehension may solve themselves. Let's mark the original sentence for rhythm. I'll put a slash for each cadence:

> For the writer / the practice / of bad writing / is harm-ful / for it results / in an inhibition / of his re-sponses / to intellectual / and imaginative / stimuli.

Every unit runs to almost the same length — da-da-dum, da-da-dum. You can see how the prepositional phrases, strung out like a snake's vertebrae, prohibit any life or vigor. The revision, while not yet "Shall I compare thee to a summer's day," at least has components of different sizes:

> Bad writing / inhibits a writer's mind / and imagina-tion.

The stress falls naturally at the end, where we want it, on "mind" and "imagination." (What would happen to this concluding stress if we said "mind and heart" instead? Would it make the concluding rhythmic unit better or worse?)

Squeezing the lard out of prose seems sometimes to liberate a natural rhythm, modest but clear, that was wait-ing to be freed. Look at this before-and-after:

BEFORE: Whereas the Wife emerges more as a victor, the
Merchant seems defeated.
AFTER: The Wife wins and the Merchant loses.

A lard factor of 47% obscures the natural modest stress on "wins" and "loses." Often rhythmic emphasis, once we are sensitive to it, will tell us what to pare away. Consider this example:

We are not surprised or shocked by her story or the manner in which she tells it.

First, *surprised* and *shocked* and *story* ring a faint alarm bell. We don't really need both verbs, since shock implies surprise. And we want the shape and rhythm of the sentence to underline the opposition of story and telling. So:

We are shocked neither by her story nor how she tells it.

"Neither . . . nor" sets up a natural contrasting rhythm, provided we keep the contrasted elements short and close together.

Often, a long string of one-syllable words will break up the rhythm, as here:

The Host's overwhelming presence in relation *to that of the rest of the* pilgrims . . .

Seven one-syllable words in a row dulls the prose bite as well as a string of jawbreakers does. Again, the villain is that string of prepositional phrases. Easy fix: "The Host overwhelms the other pilgrims." (Do you see the similarity, within the sentence, to the problem of varying length from sentence to sentence?) Once your ears have had their consciousness raised, they'll catch the easy problems as they flow from the pen — "however clever" will become "however shrewd" in the first draft — and the harder ones will seem easier to revise.

Here is a pair of ears whose consciousness badly needs raising. Try reading the passage aloud and with emphasis. Act as if the passage really said something important (what would happen to the sound if I had written "significant" here, instead of "important"?)

> Having shown the applicability of analysis of co-variance in straightforward research situations, I shall go on to indicate how several other important methodological topics can be profitably conceptualized as isomorphic in logical structure to the general linear model. . . . For several other topics as well, notably the ecological correlation fallacy, the study of compositional effects, the construction of a "standardized" index, and even the percentaging of cross tables, the logic of linear models is useful. . . .
>
> In regression analysis, as in analysis of variance, if the normality of errors assumption is made, one can analyze the variance due to the explanatory variables, ascertain its significance, and proceed in the same manner as indicated for the analysis of variance situation, and can also test hypotheses about specific values of the parameters.

Reading something like this with emphasis gives you the giggles. You cannot revise what you cannot understand, and I do not understand this. Maybe the subject simply repels any shape or rhythm. Maybe the jargon *is* the meaning. If the author had written, "Having shown how covariance analysis fits straightforward research problems, I'll now show how it fits some methodological problems," maybe scientific rigor would have been compromised. But whatever it means, your prose ought not read like a laundry list. Prose like this has become generally unreadable, has lost a whole dimension of expressibility. Notice how many polysyllabic words he uses: *applicability, analysis, covariance, straightforward, methodological, profitably, conceptualized, isomorphic, ecological correlation fallacy.* And the sentences are all about the same length.

Such prose was invented to sound scientific, to denature the writer and his subject. Statistics don't pretend to have a soul. Shakespeare, however, had one, and when people write about him after intensive study of his plays, you'd think a little joyful Shakespearian eloquence would rub off. Here are two examples which show that often it doesn't. The first is by a student, the second by a professor.

Shakespeare's *King Henry IV, Part II* is a play with a deeply ingrained tonality of languor, foreboding, and decay projected through repeated images revolving around age and death and, by association, time and disease. None of these images is exclusively independent of the others, for they intertwine throughout the play. Moreover, these images of age, death, etc. are always closely tied to the play's larger themes of order and disorder, rebellion, and the natural procession of the crown.

True to the Elizabethan philosophical outlook, the action of the play rests upon the foundation of the unnaturalness of the situation in England during the reign of Henry IV, an unnaturalness lying not only in the rebellion perpetrated against Henry by the Archbishop, Mowbry, et al., but also in the very seat of the kingdom itself, for Henry was king by virtue of usurpation from a rightful sovereign. It is into this situation that we are drawn as the play opens, and as the play is, on the level we are examining it, a chronicle of gradual disintegration, we soon develop a feel for the senses of lassitude and decay that prevail. Indeed, the first hint of this progression is contained in the Induction's description of messengers who "come tiring on" to the intriguer Northumberland's "worm-eaten hold of ragged stone," and in one messenger's description of his informant, who "seemed in running to devour the way." The descriptions conjure, at the outset, an image of a slow-devouring death or decay.

The problem as before. The prepositional phrases encourage a spontaneous monotony. The sentences seem to come in two- or three-line units or five- or six-line units. You ought, by now, to know how to fix it yourself. Try it, using the full form of our Paramedic Method, which looks like this:

1. Circle the prepositions.
2. Circle the "is" forms.
3. Ask "Who is kicking who?"
4. Put this "kicking" action in a simple (not compound) active verb.
5. Start fast — no mindless introductions.
6. Write out each sentence on a blank sheet of paper and mark off its basic rhythmic units with a / .
7. Mark off sentence lengths in the passage with a / .
8. Read the passage aloud with emphasis and feeling.

Using the PM, aim for a LF of 50%, for an emphatic short sentence or two, and for the simplest active, transitive verbs. Let the play do the acting, not you.

Now for the professor:

Attention has been confined here to the earlier comedies with the expectation that a pattern of development would show itself and a final, perfected scheme would become inducible. It is assumed here that Shakespeare did not start out as a fully competent dramatist — that he had to learn this difficult craft gradually, first by tinkering with old plays and collaborating with others. Not until he had worked with the problems of stagecraft as an apprentice did he undertake the fashioning of plays of his own contriving; even then he still relied heavily on imitation. He was still not certain of the path to follow because he had not yet evolved his own concept of the comic and perfected the stage techniques to realize it. He evolved this concept only by working it out in the course of several highly derivative plays in which he tried to master the practical matters of stage techniques, of entrances and exits, of setting up his situation, of initiating complications and conflict, of building suspense to lead to a climactic action, and of unraveling the tangled skein of action he had wound together.

Try an experiment here. We'll mark for stress and for pitch. Stress is simply the force of your voice, loud and soft; pitch is the tone of voice, high and squeaky, low and orotund. No simple and satisfactory marking systems for prose exist — this measures how hard the problem really is — but we can devise one that will mark well enough. For stress, just put a number from 1 (very weak) to 4 (very strong) above each pronounced syllable. For pitch, mark ´ for a rising pitch, – for a level one, and ˋ for a falling one. Pitch may be a problem. Americans, unlike Englishmen, tend to talk in a monotone. One of the first things a radio announcer learns is to vary the pitch of his voice. Listen to your local college station and you'll notice that the untrained announcers sound flat and unemphatic. Or compare an American and an English actor reciting Shakespeare or an English and American TV program. The difference is unmistakable. Okay, let's try marking it up.

$$\overline{2} \quad \overline{2} \quad \overline{2} \quad \overline{2} \quad \overline{2} \quad \overline{2} \quad \overline{2} \quad \acute{3} \quad \overline{2} \quad \overline{2} \quad \acute{3}\,\grave{2}\,\overline{2}$$
Attention has been confined here to the earlier

$\bar{2}$ $\bar{2}$ $\bar{2}$ $\quad$ $\bar{2}$ $\quad$ $\bar{2}$ $\bar{2}$ $\bar{2}$ $\bar{3}$ $\bar{2}$ $\quad$ $\bar{2}$ $\bar{2}$ $\bar{2}$ $\quad$ $\bar{2}$ $\quad$ $\bar{2}$
comedies with the expectation that a pattern of

$\bar{2}$ $\dot{3}$ $\grave{2}$ $\bar{2}$ $\quad$ $\bar{2}$ $\quad$ $\bar{2}$ $\bar{2}$ $\bar{2}$ $\quad$ $\bar{2}$ $\bar{2}$ $\dot{3}$ $\grave{1}$ $\quad$ $\bar{2}$ $\dot{3}$ $\grave{1}$
development would show itself and a final, perfected

$\quad$ $\bar{3}$ $\qquad$ $\bar{2}$ $\quad$ $\bar{2}$ $\bar{2}$ $\quad$ $\bar{2}$ $\dot{2}$ $\grave{1}$ $\bar{1}$ $\quad$ $\bar{2}$ $\bar{2}$ $\bar{2}$ $\quad$ $\bar{2}$ $\qquad$ $\bar{2}$
scheme would become inducible. It is assumed here

$\bar{2}$ $\quad$ $\dot{3}$ $\quad$ $\grave{2}$ $\quad$ $\bar{2}$ $\bar{2}$ $\quad$ 4 $\quad$ 4 $\bar{2}$ $\bar{2}$ $\dot{3}$ $\dot{3}$ $\quad$ $\dot{3}$ $\bar{2}$ $\bar{2}$
that Shakespeare did not start out as a fully competent

$\dot{3}$ $\grave{2}$ $\bar{2}$ $\quad$ $\bar{2}$ $\bar{1}$ $\quad$ $\bar{1}$ $\quad$ $\bar{2}$ $\quad$ 4 $\quad$ $\bar{3}$ $\quad$ $\bar{3}$ $\bar{3}$ $\bar{3}$ $\quad$ $\bar{3}$
dramatist—that he had to learn this difficult craft

$\dot{4}$ $\bar{2}$ $\bar{2}$ $\quad$ $\dot{3}$ $\bar{2}$ $\dot{2}$ $\bar{2}$ $\bar{2}$ $\quad$ $\bar{2}$ $\quad$ $\dot{3}$ $\quad$ $\bar{3}$ $\quad$ $\bar{1}$
gradually, first by tinkering with old plays and

$\bar{2}$ $\dot{3}$ $\bar{1}$ $\bar{1}$ $\bar{1}$ $\quad$ $\bar{1}$ $\quad$ $\dot{3}$ $\grave{1}$ $\quad$ $\bar{2}$ $\quad$ $\bar{2}$ $\bar{2}$ $\bar{2}$ $\quad$ $\bar{2}$ $\qquad$ $\bar{2}$
collaborating with others. Not until he had worked

$\bar{2}$ $\quad$ $\bar{2}$ $\quad$ $\dot{2}$ $\quad$ $\grave{2}$ $\quad$ $\bar{1}$ $\quad$ $\bar{2}$ $\quad$ $\bar{2}$ $\quad$ $\bar{1}$ $\bar{1}$ $\bar{2}$ $\quad$ 4 $\quad$ $\dot{4}$ $\quad$ $\bar{2}$
with the problems of stagecraft as an apprentice did

$\bar{2}$ $\quad$ $\bar{2}$ $\bar{2}$ $\dot{2}$ $\quad$ $\bar{2}$ $\quad$ $\dot{3}$ $\quad$ $\bar{2}$ $\bar{1}$ $\quad$ $\bar{1}$ $\quad$ $\bar{2}$ $\quad$ $\bar{1}$ $\bar{3}$ $\quad$ $\dot{3}$
he undertake the fashioning of plays of his own

$\bar{3}$ $\quad$ 4 $\grave{3}$ $\quad$ $\dot{3}$ $\dot{3}$ $\quad$ 4 $\quad$ $\bar{2}$ $\quad$ $\dot{2}$ $\quad$ $\bar{2}$ $\bar{2}$ $\quad$ $\dot{3}$ $\dot{3}$ $\bar{3}$ $\bar{2}$
contriving; even then he still relied heavily on

$\bar{2}$ $\bar{2}$ 4 $\grave{1}$
imitation.

What do you notice? Well, not much dynamic range, for a start — not much difference between the strong and the weak stress, high and low pitch. Such markings inevitably seem a matter of personal preference. They almost always are. All prose involves, even if it doesn't invite, personal performance. We recreate it in our mouths and ears. But the better the prose, the more clearly it invites us to do this in a certain way, issues a set of performance instructions. In this passage, the instructions are very vague. We do what we can with the monotony, but it isn't

much. If we try to impose too much rhythm on it, it begins to sound silly. I'll try to revise the professor's prose to
make this invitation a little more appealing. The revision
per the PM: break up the prepositional phrases and "is"
clusters; get back to the root verb and keep it simple;
squeeze out the lard; vary the sentence length.

Someone has told the professor that a writer should
never speak in his own person. He must never say, "I
have examined" but rather "Attention has been confined
to," never "I assume" but "It is assumed here that." How
such a silly rule got started is hard to imagine. Every sentence ought not begin with "I," obviously — you'd have a
kind of aye-aye-aye-aye Spanish folk-song chorus — but
otherwise it all depends, again, on where the action is,
who is kicking who. Don't hesitate to take credit for an action you perform. If you want to include the reader, stage
your writing as a social endeavor, say "We have now
agreed that. . .". That's fine, too. "I" and "we" imply
two different dramatic choices for expository prose,
monologue and dialogue. Choose whichever one suits
your subject and your personality. If you want to make it
sound as if your assertions came from On High, you can
use an impersonal construction — "Attention has been
confined to. . .". That's why bureaucrats are so fond of
"It has been decided that. . .". No one has done the action; hence, if it proves wrong, no one need take the
blame. Only the prose suffers. Especially, as here, the
rhythm.

So the first sentence might read:

  1̄ 1̄ 2̄ 1̄ 3́ 1́ 1̀ 1̄ 3́ 1̄1̄ 2̀ 1̄ 1̄
 I've considered here only the earlier comedies,

  2́ 1̀ 1̄ 1́ 1̄ 3́ 1̄ 1̄ 3̄ 2̄ 1̄
 hoping to find a pattern that Shakespeare would

  2̄ 2́2̀ 1̄ 1̄ 3́1̀ 2̄
 develop in the later ones.

We want the rhythm to underline this basic pattern:

> I considered . . . earlier comedy
>
> Shakespeare developed . . . later . . . ones

Every element ought to point up this parallelism.

If unqualified adjectives often bear more strongly than intensified ones ("I was angry" rather than "I tell you, I was really very angry indeed"), bald and unintroduced assertions almost always assert themselves more strongly than carefully qualified ones. Back to our early example. Better "Jim kicks Bill" than "It can be confidently asserted at this time that Jim kicks Bill." So here in the second sentence: amputate "It is assumed that" and the sentence gets going much faster. And stop after "dramatist" and you have what this passage needs the most — a short emphatic sentence: "Shakespeare did not begin as a competent dramatist" (LF 47%). I've changed "started out" to "begin" to cut the preposition, and cut "fully" on the principle just stated, that intensifying modifiers often weaken instead. As a result of all this, the sentence becomes a focal point for the argument. (I nearly wrote "for the entire argument." But how about "the sentence *focuses* the argument"?) The assumption has become what it really is — an assertion. And the sentence possesses, at last, a strategy. Mark for rhythm and you'll see that everything has been arranged to throw maximum stress on *"begin."*

What strategy should we work out for the next part of the sentence: "that he had to learn this difficult craft gradually, first by tinkering with old plays and collaborating with others." Clearly we want to underscore the parallelism between old plays and other playwrights. "He learned gradually, first by tinkering with old plays and collaborating with other playwrights." Notice how, given a sentence of its own and thinned down a bit, the assertion gains force? It no longer has to draw its vital force from a distant "assumed." Stress falls naturally on "gradually" ("natural*ly*" and "gradual*ly*" make an awkward pair — revision?) and on the "tinkering . . . old plays" / "collaborating . . . other playwrights" parallel pair.

The next sentence is mostly guff:

> Not until / he had worked / with the problems / of stage craft / as an apprentice / did he undertake / the fashioning / of plays / of his own contriving; / even then / he still relied heavily / on imitation.

The stress pattern the sentence wants to make — apprentice, own, plays, imitation — comes clear in revision:

> 1 1 3 1 2 2 2 1 4 1 1 1 1
> Only after his stagecraft apprenticeship did he
>
> 1 3 1 1 4 1 1 4 1 2 1
> write plays of his own, and even then he often
> 3 1 1
> imitated. (LF 45%)

Try revising the rest of the passage yourself. The lard factor has been running about 45%. Look for the natural rhythm, the natural pattern of stress, the natural musculature. It's there, buried in fat.

When you try to write rhythmical prose, you are inviting your reader to sing. Prose varies in how this invitation is extended. Sometimes it is totally built in. We are told *exactly* how to sing. Sometimes it depends on our already knowing a pattern of stress. And sometimes it gives us no clues at all, so that without a performance to follow as a model, we're lost. As an example of this last, take the words of a golden not-so-oldie:

> When you're weary, feeling small,
> When tears are in your eyes, I will dry them all;

I'm on your side. When times get rough
And friends just can't be found,
Like a bridge over troubled water
I will lay me down.
Like a bridge over troubled water
I will lay me down.

Pretty flat and lifeless. Write it out as prose and it would be prose. With its melody, it was a charming song, but it depends entirely on that melody for its performance. It contains no internal clues. Try this with current songs. Do some carry more performance information than others?

When we underline a word or put it in quotation marks when it is not a quotation, we're trying to add performance instructions, to tell the reader how to read. Try, with just underlining (maybe with a double underlining once or twice) and quotation marks to add performance instructions to the following passage. A Los Angeles guru is commenting on the Big Sur hippie scene of a few years ago.

— When I first got up there, it was a real romantic kind of picture. Man, it was kind of foggy. There were those really beautiful people — men, women, kids, dogs and cats, and campfires. It seemed quiet and stable. And I really felt like love was about me. I thought, "This is the place, man. It was happening. I don't have to do it. I would just kind of fit in and do my thing and that would be like a groove."

After we were there about fifteen or twenty minutes, I heard the people bitching and moaning. I listened to it for awhile and circulated around to hear more about it, and, man, I couldn't believe it. Here they were secure in their land — beautiful land, where they could be free — and all these people were doing was bitching and moaning. I thought, "Oh, shit, man! Do I have to go into this kind of shit again where I gotta step in and get heavy and get ratty and get people to start talking? Do I have to get them to be open and get in some dialogue and get some communication going and organization? What the —— is wrong with the leadership here, that this kind of state of affairs is happening? And why do I have to do it again? Man, I'm through with it. I just got through with hepatitis and double pneumonia and . . . —— it!" Then I really felt bad. (Lewis Yablonsky, *The Hippie Trip* [New York: Pegasus, 1968], p. 91.)

This is speech, for a start. And hippie speech, heavily syncopated speech, sliding quickly over interim syllables from heavy stress to heavy stress: "first," "romantic," "foggy," "really," "love." Once you know the syncopated pattern, it is easy to mark up a passage like this. But if you don't know the pattern? Imagine yourself a foreigner trying to read this passage with a natural emphasis. It does sometimes give clues. "This is the *place, man.* It was *happening. I* don't have to do it." The arrangement of the words underscores the sense — the scene has become the actor and the actor the scene. So, too, the alliterative repetition of "go into," "gotta step in," "get heavy," "get ratty," "get people," gives us a clear performance clue. But the passage by itself does not include a full guide to its performance.

How *can* prose include such a guide? It does so often by patterns of repetition, balance, antithesis, and parallelism. The following example comes from Lord Brougham (1778–1868), a famous Parliamentary orator, in his speech defending Queen Caroline in the divorce proceedings George IV had brought against her. This kind of prose seems fulsome to us, but notice how many performance clues it contains.

But, my lords, I am not reduced to this painful necessity. I feel that if I were to touch this branch of the case now, until any event shall afterwards show that unhappily I am deceiving myself — I feel that if I were now to approach the great subject of recrimination, I should seem to give up the higher ground of innocence on which I rest my cause; I should seem to be justifying when I plead Not Guilty; I should seem to argue in extenuation and in palliation of offences, or levities, or improprieties, the least and the lightest of which I stand here utterly to deny. For it is false, as has been said — it is foul and false as those have dared to say, who, pretending to discharge the higher duties to God, have shown that they know not the first of those duties to their fellow-creatures — it is foul, and false, and scandalous in those who have said (and they know that it is so who have dared to say) that there are improprieties admitted in the conduct of the Queen. I deny that the admission has been made. I contend that the evidence does not prove them. I will show you that the evidence disproves them. One admission, doubtless, I do make; and let my learned friends who are of counsel for the Bill take all the benefit of it, for it is all that they have proved by their evidence.

Several powerful variables contend in a prose like this. The patterning aims above all to establish a tone of high seriousness. But look at it simply for performance clues. It tells us exactly how it ought to be performed. Shape and Sound coincide. It builds to a climactic central assertion and then tapers off. Perhaps a diagram will help:

    But, my lords,
I am not reduced to this painful necessity.
I feel that if
I were to touch this branch of the case now, until
    any event shall afterwards shows that unhappily

I am deceiving myself —
I feel that if
I were now to approach the great subject of
                recrimination,
I should seem to give up the higher ground of
                innocence on which
I rest my cause;
I should seem to be justifying when
I plead Not Guilty;
I should seem to argue in extenuation
                and in palliation of
              offences, or improprieties,
              the least and
              the lightest of which
   I stand here utterly to deny.
For it is false   as has been said
    it is foul and false   as those have dared to say
        who pretending to discharge
           the high duties to God
        have shown that they know not
           the first of those duties to their fellow men
        it is foul, and false, and scandalous
              in those who have said
           (and they know that it is so
              who have dared to say)
      THAT THERE ARE IMPROPRIETIES ADMITTED IN THE
          CONDUCT OF THE QUEEN
I deny that the admission has been made;
I contend that the evidence does not prove them;
I will show you that the evidence disproves them.
One admission, doubtless, I do make
    and let my learned friends who are
        of counsel for the Bill
Take *all* the benefit of *it,* for *it* is *all* that they have
                proved by their evidence.

Notice how the conclusion is handled? He uses a chiasmus (an *ab:ba* pattern) to fold the last clause back up upon itself and then uses the last prepositional phrase to end the whole rhythmic unit. And the main pattern stands clear. First a series of repetitive hammer-blow assertions; next a set of balanced assertions and rebuttals; then the central point; then a short return to the first pattern and a short return to the second; then the final chiasmus.

We don't write prose like this any more, but whether you relish it as I do or not, you ought to try in your own writing to give equally good performance instructions. For, again, that is what sentence rhythm is — a series of instructions for how your sentence should be performed.

Here are some exercises. Try to cure their problems of sound and give them some shape and rhythm.

1. The reality which Shakespeare tries to create is a psychological one rather than a physical or dramatic one.

2. Her frailties and shortcomings were human and humorless.

3. Elsewhere, I have sought to show that the chief contribution to philosophy of Cassirer's analysis of the humanistic disciplines is that, admitting the ubiquity of natural process in all experience, he goes on to demonstrate that questions of logic, of definition, are necessarily prior to any intelligent, scientifically soluble, questions as to the emergence of such thoughts *as products of nature,* thus making obvious the all-too-common tendency of naturalistic philosophies to embrace uncritically this or that theory purporting to prove that meaning and form are identical with the natural processes, or cooperations of processes, which maintain them and bring them into being; for, as such, they are no more the thinking process than "what is seen" is the seeing process; they are *merely* the logical or formal aspect of such supporting and encompassing existential situations.

4. The obvious effect of such a range of reference is to assure the audience of the author's range of learning and intellect.

5. The model for Bacon's Essays is the condensed, aphoristic manner characteristic of Seneca. One problem that Bacon does not completely overcome, however, is the lack of smoothness created by successive use of aphorisms.

6. Although Chaucer pokes fun at the courtly love convention and derives humor from its excesses, it cannot be denied that the attitude of the author toward the love code remains at the same time serious and is marked by pathos.

7. I overcome dictionary deficiency by seeking a definition in the writings by great thinkers.

8. The issue of satisfaction with a verdict is the substance of a previous legal decision by Pantagruel, as it is also in this trial.

9. If, then, divination by dice is evil, one may well ask why judgment by the same means is praiseworthy. However, the assumption that the fall of dice may be consulted and interpreted as being a manifestation of divine will is in contradiction to an earlier pronouncement by Pantagruel on the foolishness and wickedness of divination by dice.

10. It is my intent to point out how by the time of Defoe, Dickens, Goethe and Goldsmith the conscious idea of the family as a unit has been so accepted in civilization that it appears in the major works we have used in a most subtle form.

11. Here are four successive drafts of a passage from a paper submitted to a graduate school of business. Explain why the author made each change. Consider not only matters of rhythm but all the techniques of revision we've discussed up to now.

A PILOT STUDY OF THE FARMER RICHMAN MODEL AS
A PREDICTIVE OF THE RELATIVE PERFORMANCE OF

Research Objective

The research described in this paper was undertaken to examine the prospect of a contemplated European field trip comprising a year or more of rigorous data collection, analysis and subsequent dissertation writing. The field trip, if undertaken, would involve (a) data collection at the scene of subcontract activity (examination of public and subcontractor records, interviewing with representatives of the several layers of subcontractor organizations, and questionnaires for subcontractor personnel and civil servants, for a broad data base) at the eight European subcontractors of the Hughes Aircraft Company Intelsat IV Program, and (b) assessment of these data using the Farmer Richman Model.

Prior to making a commitment to time-consuming, expensive, and career-disruptive European field work, therefore, the present preliminary and local research was undertaken as a pilot effort to determine if the Intelsat IV Program can usefully be examined in the context of the Farmer Richman Model. That is, whether the Farmer Richman Model can contribute to an understanding of how to improve management and managerial effectiveness (as these terms are used in the Model) in programs such as the Intelsat IV Program.

The immediate objective of this study, therefore, is to assess the predictive capacity of the Farmer Richman Model with respect to the Intelsat IV Program and, in particular, the Model's ability to predict the relative management and managerial effectiveness of the several Intelsat IV subcontractors.

SECOND DRAFT

FARMER RICHMAN MODEL PREDICTIVENESS: HUGHES
AIRCRAFT COMPANY INTELSAT IV PROGRAM

Research Objective

I undertook this pilot study to decide whether to embark on a European field trip comprising a year's data collection, analysis, and subsequent dissertation writing. The field trip would involve data collecting at the eight subcontractor plants, examining company records, and interviewing subcontractor representative employees, and data collection, examining public records and questioning civil servants to obtain a broad data base. My objective would be to collect data to assess the predictiveness of the Farmer Richman Model.

Prior to making this commitment to time-consuming, expensive, and career-disruptive European field work, I engaged in preliminary, local research to examine two possibilities. The first, whether the Intelsat IV Program provides a means to test Farmer Richman predictiveness. The second, an outgrowth of the first, whether the Farmer Richman Model contributes to improved management and managerial effectiveness (as these terms are used in the Model) in programs such as the Intelsat IV Program.

My objective, therefore, is to assess Farmer Richman Model predictiveness with respect to the Intelsat IV Program and, in particular, to assess the Model's ability to predict the relative subcontractor "management and managerial effectiveness" of Intelsat IV subcontractors.

THIRD DRAFT

FARMER RICHMAN MODEL PREDICTIVENESS: HUGHES AIRCRAFT COMPANY INTELSAT IV PROGRAM

Research Objective

I undertook this pilot study to decide whether to go on a European field trip comprising more than a year's data collecting and analysis, preparatory to writing a dissertation on international management. During such a trip, I would collect data at eight subcontractor plants, examining company records, and interviewing subcontractor employees. I would collect data by examining public records and questioning civil servants. My objective would be to collect data to assess Farmer Richman Model predictiveness in a multinational environment.

Before committing myself to time-consuming, expensive, and career disruptive European field work, I conducted preliminary, local research. This paper describes the local investigation and its results. My objective is to test the Model's ability to predict relative "management and managerial effectiveness" of Intelsat IV subcontractors.

FOURTH DRAFT

FARMER RICHMAN MODEL PREDICTIVENESS: HUGHES AIRCRAFT COMPANY INTELSAT IV PROGRAM

Research Objective

I undertook this pilot study to decide whether to go to Europe for a year to collect data, before writing an international management dissertation. During this field trip, I would visit eight Intelsat IV subcontractor plants, examining company records and interviewing subcontractor employees; I would examine public records and question civil servants; and I would collect data at the Hughes European Program Office and the subcontractor supplier plants. All this data would then be used to assess Farmer Richman Model predictiveness in a multinational environment.

Before committing my family and myself to the inconvenience imposed by European field work, I conducted preliminary local research. I wanted to see whether the Model could predict *relative* Intelsat IV subcontractor "management and managerial effectiveness." This paper describes the results.

12. What do the following revisions try to do?

ORIGINAL

Let us first examine part of what is, in my opinion, the correct interpretation of the Parable of the Laborers in the Vineyard. In the exegesis of any passage of the Bible, it is fundamental that one must understand the context of the passage as well as the content. The context in which the Parable of the Laborers in the Vineyard is found plainly shows that the subject being dealt with is the different degrees of eternal reward in heaven.

REVISION

What does the parable really mean? In Biblical exegesis, context matters as well as content. The context here plainly shows that the subject is the different degrees of heavenly reward.

ORIGINAL

There is, however, another way to view this digression. From the moment when Venus grabbed the horse's reins and dragged Adonis off, we have seen a reversal in the traditional male and female roles. Simply, Venus is the pursuer, Adonis is the pursued. This theme is continually supported through imagery.

REVISION

This digression works a second way. From the moment Venus grabs the horse's reins and drags Adonis off under her arm, the traditional sex roles are reversed. Venus pursues; Adonis flees.

CHAPTER FOUR

Voice and Sight Feedback

Voice: The "I mean, like, you know" plague

The 1970's may go down in history as the time when everybody said "You know?" and nobody knew. I've in my files an article from the *Los Angeles Times,* entitled "Curing Contagious Phrase Epidemic." It's dated August 1971. Today "like, you know" still thrives. It promises to be a ten-year plague at least, but when it finally burns itself out, the high point may prove to have been Mark Spitz lecturing some journalists visiting him on his sailboat:

> "First," he said, "if you gotta, you know, throw up or anything, I mean, get seasick, go to the back of the boat and lean over the low side so you don't, you know, do it up here and get it all over, you know." (Charles T. Powers, "Spitz Sets Sail on a Sea of Green," *Los Angeles Times,* April 26, 1975)

As the chronicling reporter nicely translated it: "Spitz's first law of seamanship: Never toss your cookies into the wind." Or, more likely, "Never, I mean, toss, like, your, you know, cookies into the, uh, wind."

The method for curing this spasmodic verbal tic suggests itself easily enough. Listen to yourself speak. As a first step, listen — really listen — to other people speak.

If you are not used to doing this, make some tapes. A cassette recorder can tell you the whole story. Alternately, keep a ⊬⊬⊬ count of how many times you hear "I mean," "like" or "you know" in, say, a ten-minute period. I have counted twenty in one minute.

These continual interruptions act, like TV commercials, to break the attention span into fragments, fragments unrelated to sense or syntax. Like a self-imposed stutter, they prevent any continuous, much less shaped or rhythmic, discourse. People deep in the habit seem possessed by a mindless demon, a compulsive verbal hiccough. They substitute for the expressive power of language a specific request for common understandings ("you know?") and common analogies ("like"), both of which presumably lie beyond language.

The phenomenal growth of this verbal spasm testifies to more than its own unattractiveness. It bespeaks a generation inattentive to language and uncomfortable in its use. Deaf, blind, and impatient. This inattention concerns anyone writing or reading prose because it has caused our current crisis in written utterance. "You know?" supplies the voiced equivalent of the implicit plea offered by the shapeless, rhythmless, obese prose we have been examining — "Please understand me, even though neither I nor you can really understand what, if anything, I have said." It requests a tacit agreement to be mindless together.

Americans ignore their speech for the same reason they ignore their writing. Words don't matter. Only the idea. The "you know" disease results. When you cease to notice the verbal surface, you commit yourself to attitudinal communication. You can talk to your fellow men, that is, only in the way you talk to your dog. *What* you say, if anything, doesn't matter. Tone of voice is all. Try calling your dog when she doesn't want to come in. You'll be forced into the *tones* of endearment, even if *what* you say is, "Scarlet, if you *ever do* come in this door I'm going to take this newspaper and beat you from one end of the house to the other." Written prose, however, has no natural tonal language like this at its disposal. Getting the tone, the attitudinal coloration, back into it constitutes a final accomplishment, not a natural birthright. Give up its conceptual ingredient and you end up with the kind of prose increasingly prevalent in our own time, prose less *incorrect* than meaningless.

Americans have always been natural romantics. Natural is best. Premeditated speech has to be somehow insincere speech. Snobbish. Undemocratic. Fake. We've grown, as a result, into a nation of Tin Ears. Without trying to solve the paradox that only artifice is natural to man, surely the therapy is simply to listen. America is still very rich in regional and ethnic accents. The flat Tennessee mountain accent, the Georgia drawl, the New England accents from South Shore Massachusetts to old-fashioned Vermont, comprise a treasure chest we scarcely notice. And, like other regional differences, they are disappearing. We ought to cherish them. They are fun in themselves, and they make us listen to how we speak. We'll end up, if we're self-conscious about our speaking, with styles as various as our personalities instead of with the inane commonality of "You know?"

A speaking voice both publicly declares the personality and forms it. The voice provides a perfect model, in an inevitable and inevitably public context, for the mutual influence of writer and writing. If you can become self-conscious about your voice, you'll begin to have a genuine voice of your own. And once you have it, you can try to put it into your prose. People will hear you in your prose because they'll be a you to hear. You won't have to keep asking people if they know. They'll know without your asking.

The self-teaching techniques here are easy. Record yourself and the conversation around you and then transcribe and analyze it. "You know" is only the way in, not the whole story. Do you speak in a monotone? Always interrupt? Say one thing but, by your tone of voice, mean another? What has been said about rhythm, shape, and emphasis holds for speaking even more than writing. Try marking up your own transcribed speech. What does it look like? Can you find the idiosyncratic patterns of genuine personality? Are they effective or simply quirky? The crisis in writing has many causes, but at its center stands a crisis in self-consciousness. You can use speech to show yourself what stylistic self-consciousness can amount to. Radio and TV announcers usually have their idiosyncrasies trained out of them, but the callers on telephone shows don't, and neither, often, do the guests on talk shows and interview programs. Record and analyze them. No phonological training is required. Just listen. You might then want to try voice training, but you may just find yourself thinking before you speak. This kind of self-consciousness can do nothing but good to your prose.

We've seen how sentences become shapeless when the voice goes out of them. Prose that is not *voiced* becomes shapeless and unemphatic in the same way that an unexercised muscle loses its tone. And it works the other way, too. If we do not look *at* a piece of prose, try to perform it, we'll cease to hear real voices, our own and others, when we speak. Writing and speaking form a spiral. If they intensify each other, the spiral goes up. If they don't, each drives the other down.

Sight: Typing

Stylistic self-consciousness can be visual too. That's why if you are serious about improving your prose, you must know how to type. For revision, the typewriter is mightier than the pen. Some people can compose at the typewriter and others can't, but we all need to type up what we've written before we can revise it. When typesetting was cheap authors could revise from a set of galley proofs.

But the typewriter does nearly as well, whether or not your prose will finally see print. The typewriter distances prose and it does it quickly. By depersonalizing our price-less prose, a typescript shows it to us as seen through a stranger's eyes. It tells us what it looks like, literally how it "shapes up." No single bad writing habit is so powerful as the habit of typing an essay only when you are ready to turn it in. Correct the handwritten manuscript by all means, but then type a draft and revise that. A typed ver-sion makes everything clearer, especially problems of sen-tence shape, rhythm, and emphasis. Typing will also per-mit a friend to read your prose back to you, with all the revelations that usually brings. And a freshly typed draft, by wiping the slate clean of previous changes, allows a new beginning. You have revised the prose. The fresh draft allows that prose, with its look of crisp finality, to convince you if it can. If, after you have applied our PM it still looks good, then it may be getting better. The typed draft represents the central mechanical stage in the cre-ative oscillation we go through, that back-and-forth move-ment in which first we suggest things to the prose and then it suggests things to us. "How do I know what I think until I see what I write?" enshrines a profound truth, and the typed draft allows this process to work most ef-ficiently. So if you don't know how to type, you must learn. For anyone who wants to write, typing is not a frill. It is essential.

Typing solves some minor problems as well. Para-graphing, for a start. So much is made of paragraphing and THE TOPIC SENTENCE that it seems sacrilegious to think paragraphing largely a visual contrivance, a typo-graphical convention. Yet it is. Paragraphing for a double-column format, a journalist's column, means one thing; for an ordinary book, another. How long a paragraph should be depends on how it strikes the eye. Paragraph-ing must correspond to a division of sense, but you'll be surprised how flexible this sense division can be.

Try not paragraphing at all next time you write something. Type up the first draft the same way. Then decide on a sensible paragraph length for an 8½ x 11 page — eight or ten lines, say — and see how closely you come to finding sense breaks that correspond to that length. Absolute limits exist, of course. One-sentence paragraphs are a contradiction in terms, since the paragraph is the next larger prose division after the sentence. Pints should not equal quarts. Nor should a paragraph normally run longer than a full page. Two or three paragraphs per page is a good rule. A newspaper column can tolerate more, though the common journalistic habit of one- or two-line paragraphs is silly.

The topic sentence is seldom the *sine qua non* composition texts make it out to be. Forget about it and get on with what you have to say. If your argument has any shape at all, it will mark its own stages clearly, whether they occur one to a paragraph, or more, or less. And if the argument does not have any shape, typing will make that embarassingly clear. Then get out the scissors and paste and rearrange. Don't be embarrassed. We all do it. Typing just makes it much easier.

CHAPTER FIVE

The Official Style

Up to now we've been analyzing particular stylistic elements — shape, rhythm, emphasis. We've seen, in the process, that these elements are interrelated, that they seem to proceed from the same aesthetic, constitute a common style. In the examples we've been revising, we've been in effect translating from The Official Style into plain English. Now we are going to do this directly, focus on The Official Style as an exercise in stylistic analysis and translation. At the same time, we'll try, instead of simply condemning The Official Style, to ask how and why it has come about, how it works in the world.

Students of style have traditionally distinguished three basic levels — high, middle, low. The content of these categories varied somewhat, but usually the high style was a formal and ornamental style for a solemn and ritualized occasion, the low style was the loose and sloppy intercourse of daily life, and the middle style stood somewhere in between. Since World War II, American prose has worked a pronounced variation on this enduring pattern. We've seen what has happened to the low style. It has disintegrated into a series of I-mean-like-you-know spastic tics. And since we have come to suspect both fancy language and formal ceremony in America, we have come to suspect the high style, too. As a substitute, we've clasped to our bosoms The Official Style. The Official Style is often stigmatized as bureaucratese or jargon and often is both. But it is a genuine style, and one that reflects the genuine bureaucratization of American life. It has its own rules and its own reasons, and anyone writing prose nowadays in America must come to know both. The Official Style runs from school days to retirement. As soon as you realize that you live "in a system," whether P.S. 41, the University of California, or the Department of Agriculture, you start developing The Official Style. Used unthinkingly, it provides the quickest tip-off that you have become system-sick, and look at life only through the system's eyes. It is a scribal style, ritualized, formulaic, using a private vocabulary to describe a particular kind of world. And it is, increasingly, the only kind of prose style America ever sees. It is also, along with the social changes that sponsor it, the main reason for our prose problem. The low style has dissolved, the high style has hardened and dehydrated, and the middle style has simply evaporated. The Official Style threatens to replace all three.

If you can analyze, write, and translate it, maybe you can find your niche in The System without losing your soul to it. For you may have to write in The Official Style but you don't have to think in it. If you are the first on the scene after the car has missed the curve, climbed the hedge and ended up on your lawn, you won't ask the driver, as did the policeman, "How, uh, did you achieve this configuration?"

Sometimes you can see The Official Style seizing its prey like a boa constrictor and gradually squeezing the life out of it. Here's a student feeling its grip.

Twelve-year-old boys like to fight. Consequently, on several occasions I explained to them the negative aspects of fighting. Other responsibilities included keeping them dry (when near the creek or at times of rain), seeing that they bathed, attending to any minor wounds they acquired, and controlling their mischievous behavior. Another responsibility was remaining patient with the children.

The first sentence says simply what it has to say. The second sentence starts to sound like a report. It strives for a needless explicitness ("on several occasions") and it aims for a pseudoscientific neutrality of description, "the negative aspects of fighting." To remain on the same stylistic level as the first sentence, it ought to read, "So, I often told them to stop." "Other responsibilities included" is the language of a job-description. The frantic scramble of a summer camp is being viewed through a personnel form. The prose is scary as well as stilted because life has been reduced to something that will fit in a file cabinet. Only on official forms do small boys "acquire minor wounds" or counselors "attend" them. In life, they cut themselves and you give them a Band-Aid. In life, you keep them out of the creek and out of the rain, instead of "keeping them dry (when near the creek or at times of rain)." And, instead of "controlling their mischievous behavior," you make them behave or even give them a kick in the pants. As for "Another responsibility was remaining patient with the children," that translates into, "I had to keep my temper." If the writer had stayed on the level he began with, he would have written:

> Twelve-year-old boys like to fight. Often, I had to stop them. And I had to keep them out of the rain, and the creek, and mischief generally. I had to give out Band-Aids and keep my temper.

Why didn't he? You don't write The Official Style by nature. It has to be learned. Why did he fall into it here? He was applying for something. And you apply for something — in this case, admission to medical school — on a form. And a form requires an official style. The Official

Style. It makes what you've done sound important and, still more important than important, *official*.

Ever since George Orwell's famous essay "Politics and the English Language" (1946), The Official Style has been interpreted as a vast conspiracy to soften our minds and corrupt our political judgment. Social science jargon has been seen as pure hokum, an attempt to seem more scientific than you are. And the language of the Pentagon bureaucrats during the Vietnam war often seemed to combine the worst of these two worlds. The Orwell conspiracy theory is sometimes true, but not the whole truth. We all want to fit in, to talk the language of the country. This desire is what keeps society glued together. So the impulses that attract us to The Official Style are not always perverse or depraved. Just the opposite. They are the primary social impulses. And so when we analyze The Official Style, we're really talking about how we live now, about our *society* as well as our prose, about how to survive in The System. What does the prose tell us about the society?

Well, it is a euphemistic society, for a start. It thinks of every town dump as a "Sanitary Landfill Site," every mentally retarded child as "exceptional," every dog catcher as an "animal welfare officer." Society may have its pains and problems, but language can sugarcoat them.

The second rule in this society is "Keep your head down. Don't assert anything you'll have to take the blame for. Don't, if you can help it, assert anything at all." Anthony Sampson has culled a few examples of this super-caution from a British Civil Service version of The Official Style and supplied plain language translations.

> We hope that it is fully appreciated that . . .
> > You completely fail to realize that . . .
>
> Greater emphasis should be laid on . . .
> > You haven't bothered to notice . . .

We have the impression that insufficient study has
been given to . . .
No one has considered . . .

Our enquiry seemed to provide a welcome opportunity for discussions of problems of this kind . . .
No one had thought of that before . . .

We do not think that there is sufficient aware-
ness . . .
There is ignorance . . .

There has been a tendency in the past to overestimate
the possibilities of useful short-term action in public
investment . . .
You should look ahead . . .

There should be an improvement in the arrangements to enable ministers to discharge their collective
responsibility . . .
The cabinet should work together . . .

(*Anatomy of Britain,* New York: Harper & Row, 1962)

The main rule is clear. Don't make an assertion you can
get tagged with later. It may come back to haunt you. So
never write "I think" or "I did." Keep the verbs passive
and impersonal: "It was concluded that" or "appropriate
action was initiated on the basis of systematic discussion
indicating that." Often, as with politicians being inter-
viewed on TV, The Official Style aims deliberately at saying nothing at all, but saying it in the required way. Or at
saying the obvious in a seemingly impressive way. The Official Stylist seems in control of everything but responsible
for nothing. Thus a congressman, instead of saying that
the government will listen to consumer complaints, says
that it will "review existing mechanisms of consumer

input, thruput, and output and seek ways of improving these linkages via consumer consumption channels." The computer language of input, output, and interface has been seized upon by The Official Style as a kind of poetic diction, a body of sacred and intrinsically beautiful metaphors. Thus, a U.S. senator indicted on bribery charges does not ask the advice of his friends. He instead is "currently receiving personal and political input from my supporters and friends throughout the state."

It is often hard to tell with The Official Style how much is self-conscious put-on and how much real ineptitude, genuine system-sickness. Students often say that the length and physical weight of their papers is more important than what they say, yet it is not only in school that papers are graded thus. Here is a famous Washington lawyer, talking about legal language.

> In these days when every other type of professional report, good or poor, is dressed up in a lovely ringed and colored plastic binder, some people still are prone to judge legal performance quantitatively by verbal volume. Thirty years ago two of us answered a difficult and intricate legal problem by concisely writing: "Gentlemen, after examining the statute in your state, all analogous statutes, and all of the cases, we have concluded that what you want to do is lawful." That client was not happy; he went down to Wall Street, got the same opinion backed by thirty turgid typewritten pages, and felt much more comfortable. (Quoted in Joseph C. Guelden, *The Superlawyers* [New York: Dell, 1972], p. 306)

It is not only schoolteachers who find length and obscurity impressive.

Here is another example of The Official Style, social science dialect:

A policy decision inexorably enforced upon a depression-prone individual whose posture in respect to his total psychophysical environment is rendered antagonistic by apprehension or by inner-motivated disinclination for ongoing participation in human existence is the necessity for effectuating a positive selection between two alternative programs of action, namely, (a) the continuance of the above-mentioned existence irrespective of the dislocations, dissatisfactions, and disabilities incurred in such a mode, or (b) the voluntary termination of such existence by self-initiated instrumentality, irrespective in this instance of the undetermined character of the subsequent environment, if any, in which the subject may be positioned as an end result of this irrevocable determination.

Serious or a joke? A joke. In fact, one of the clever variations on common clichés devised by Richard D. Altick in his *A Preface to Critical Reading* to illustrate The Official Style. The text varied is, of course, "To be or not to be, that is the question."

Now, by contrast, someone genuinely system-sick. No joke. He has come to *think* in The Official Style. A librarian, of all people, he is trying to tell us that some books will be kept behind the desk, others put on shelves outside:

Primarily, this reorganization and the related changes are designed to facilitate the processing of lists. Placing responsibility for the processing of lists directly within the Technical Processing Division will provide a smoother and more efficient work flow, which we anticipate will result in your materials becoming more readily available. Second, it will allow optimum access to the collection, and third, provide a browsing capability formerly denied users of reserved materials.

For this new system to be successful we need your full cooperation. The attached Guidelines for Reserve Lists details the manner in which we need lists prepared. Essentially, we are requesting that required readings be distinguished from optional readings. Required readings stipulated for two hour use will be placed on closed reserve in an area behind the circulation desk. Required readings circulating for one day will remain in the open stacks; however, as opposed to regular open stack materials, these books will be marked to indicate one day use. Optional readings will circulate for regular loan periods.

In the past, the primary means for soliciting faculty input for acquiring materials for the College Library has been through reserve lists. It is our desire that optimal reading lists for undergraduates will be an effective mechanism for faculty to identify materials for the library's open stack collection.

It is our hope that you will find these changes mutually beneficial for yourselves and your students.

Your cooperation and assistance in this matter will be greatly appreciated.

If he translated this into language less wordy, shapeless, pompous, and pretentious, he might make things clearer to the faculty but he would be only a librarian, not a bureaucratic witch doctor. He would be simply putting the books out on the shelf, not "providing a browsing capability."

You must, if you are to write prose in an America and a world fated to become ever more bureaucratic, learn how to use The Official Style, even perhaps how to enjoy it, without becoming imprisoned by it. You must manage to remember who is on first base, even if often you will not want to let on that you know.

Long ago, La Rochefoucauld talked about a grave manner as "a mysterious carriage of the body to cover defects of the mind." The Official Style has elevated this into an article of faith. Here is a sociological sample collected by Malcolm Cowley, with his translation:

> In effect, it was hypothesized, that certain physical data categories including housing types and densities, land use characteristics, and ecological location constitute a scalable content area. This could be called a continuum of residential desirability. Likewise, it was hypothesized that several social data categories, describing the same census tracts, and referring generally to the social stratification system of the city, would also be scalable. This scale would be called a continuum of socio-economic status. Thirdly, it was hypothesized that there would be a high positive correlation between the scale types on each continuum.

Here's the translation:

> Rich people live in big houses set farther apart than those of poor people. By looking at an aerial photograph of any American city, we can distinguish the richer from the poorer neighborhoods. ("Sociological Habit Patterns In Linguistic Transmogrification," *The Reporter,* Sept. 20, 1956)

Such prose seems to aim at being scientific but actually wants to be priestly, to cast a witch doctor's spell. To translate the prose into a plain style — that is, to revise it into ordinary English — breaks the spell and defeats the purpose.

We face, then, the euphemistic habit yet again, though on a larger scale. The Official Style always wants to make things seem better than they are, more mysterious and yet somehow more controlled, more inevitable. It strives, at all times, both to disarm and to impress us. It suggests that it sees the world differently — sees, even, a different world. It suggests that those who see in this way form a happy band of brothers. Now such a use of language does not, to students of literature, sound unfamiliar. It is called poetic diction. And this is what The Official Style amounts to — poetry. The first rule about poetry is that you cannot translate it into prose without destroying its real meaning. And here we come to the central problem with The Official Style. There is no point in reproaching it for not being clear. It does not want to be clear. It wants to be poetic. It seems to be distant and impersonal, but it really is just the opposite. At its best, it wants to tell you how it *feels* to be an official, to project the sense of numinous self-importance officialdom confers. It wants to make a prosaic world mysterious.

I know, I know. It doesn't do it very well. But that's not the point. Until we see what it is trying to do, we can neither understand it nor translate it with any pleasure. Maybe a comparison will make the point clearer. Here is a little glossary of poetic diction which Alexander Pope compiled for a satire on false poetic sublimity called *Peri Bathos* (1728). He gives first the ordinary language equivalent and then the poetic diction.

> Who knocks at the Door?
> For whom thus rudely pleads my loud-tongued gate
> That he may enter? . . .

> See who is there?
> Advance the fringed curtains of thy eyes,
> And tell me who comes yonder. . . .

> Shut the Door.
> The wooden guardian of our privacy
> Quick on its axle turn. . . .

> Bring my clothes.
> Bring me what Nature, tailor to the *Bear,*
> To *Man* himself denied: She gave me Cold,
> But would not give me Clothes. . . .
>
> Light the Fire.
> Bring forth some remnant of the *Promethean* theft,
> Quick to expand th' inclement air congealed
> By *Boreas'* rude breath. . . .
>
> Snuff the Candle.
> Yon Luminary amputation needs,
> Thus shall you save its half-extinguished life.
>
> Uncork the Bottle, and chip the Bread.
> Apply thine engine to the spongy door,
> Set *Bacchus* from his glassy prison free,
> And strip white *Ceres* of her nut-brown coat.

Here is another glossary, an unintentional self-satire this time, issued by the U.S. Office of Education (1971). Again, first the ordinary term and then the poetic diction.

ACTIVITY — Allocation of personnel and logistic resources to accomplish an identifiable objective. Activities constitute the basis for defining personnel assignments and for scheduling system operations.

ANALYSIS — The splitting of an entity into its constituent parts, and the determination of relations among the parts and groups of the components.

DEVELOPMENT — Production and refinement of a system or a product through trial-revision until it accomplishes its specified objectives.

FUNCTIONS — Those things (actions) that must be done to accomplish the overall job are referred to as functions.

IMPLEMENT — To carry out. To fulfill. To give practical effect to and ensure of actual fulfillment by concrete measures.

IMPROVEMENT — Enhanced performance on any important dimension without detriment to the other essential dimensions.

MISSION — The job to be done, be it a product, a completed service, or a change in the condition of something or somebody.

NEED — A discrepancy or differential between "what is" and "what should be" (i.e., "what is required" or "what is desired"). In educational planning, "need" refers to problems rather than solutions, to the student "product" rather than to the resources for achieving that product, to the ends of education rather than to the means for attaining those ends.

OBJECTIVES — That toward which effort is directed. An intent statement and prediction for which a procedure is developed and resources allocated with a specific time frame and a measurable product signaling attainment.

PLANNING CAPABILITY OR PLANNING COMPETENCE — The organizational, procedural, technological, and support arrangements by which an agency has the capacity to apply problem-solving processes to any problem that it may face.

TASKS — Elements of a function that, when performed by people and things in proper sequential order, will or should resolve the parent function. Tasks may be performed by people, equipment, or people/equipment combination. (Robert A. Watson, "Making Things Perfectly Clear," *Saturday Review,* July 24, 1971)

This bureaucratic glossary was issued in the name of clarity but aims obviously at something else entirely, at a playful, poetic, ornamental use of language. Those who use The Official Style seldom acknowledge the paradox, but you must learn to see it if you are not to make grotesque mistakes. Clarity is the last thing The Official Style really wants to create and, if you find yourself in a bureaucratic context, the last thing *you* want to create. If you are writing a government report, a paper in sociology, or a grant-proposal in education, writing it in plain English will be disastrous. You may well want, in marshalling your thoughts, to write out an ordinary-language version. But you must then translate it into The Official Style. You must, that is, learn to read, write, and translate The Official Style as if it were a foreign language. Play games with it by all means, but don't get fooled by it.

Bureaucrats have, in the last few years, begun to do just this—play games with it. One government official, Philip Broughton, created something called the "Systematic Buzz Phrase Projector." It consists of three columns of words:

column 1	*column 2*	*column 3*
0. integrated	0. management	0. options
1. total	1. organizational	1. flexibility
2. systematized	2. monitored	2. capability
3. parallel	3. reciprocal	3. mobility
4. functional	4. digital	4. programming
5. responsive	5. logistical	5. concept
6. optional	6. transitional	6. time-phase
7. synchronized	7. incremental	7. projection
8. compatible	8. third-generation	8. hardware
9. balanced	9. policy	9. contingency

(*Newsweek*, May 6, 1968)

You think of any three numbers, 747 say, and then read off the corresponding words, "synchronized digital projection." It is a device to generate verbal ornament, a machine for poetic diction. Try making up a version for whatever dialect of The Official Style you need to write — sociological, educational, psychoanalytic. Not only will it lend new resonance and authority to your prose, it will act as a multiplier, increasing length and weight. It also acts as a mechanical muse, generates inspiration. Produce a phrase by the three-number procedure, invent a sentence for it, and then spend a paragraph or two reflecting on what it might mean. Invent a reality to which the phrase can refer.

The basic elements of The Official Style ought by now to stand clear. (1) It is built on *nouns,* vague, general, nouns. These are usually of Latin deriva*tion,* "shun" words like fixa*tion,* devia*tion,* func*tion,* construc*tion,* educa*tion,* organiza*tion.* (2) These are often, as in the game, modified by adjectives made up for other nouns like them, as in "incremental throughput" or "functional input." (3) All action is passive and impersonal. No active intransitive verbs and no direct objects. Never "I decided to fire him" but "It has been determined that that individual's continued presence in the present personnel configuration would tend to the detriment of the ongoing operational efficiency of the organizational unit in which the individual is currently employed." (4) Nothing is called by its ordinary name. You don't decide to bomb a town; instead, "It has been determined to maintain an aggressive and operational attack posture." You don't set up an office, you "initiate an ongoing administrative facility." (5) The status quo is preserved even in syntax. All motion is converted into stasis. The Official Style denies, as much as possible, the reality of action. You don't dislike someone, you "maintain a posture of disapproval toward" him. You don't decide to hire someone, you "initiate the hiring situation."

These rules allow you to translate into and out of The Official Style. As a help, here are some translation exercises. Some come from notable Official Stylists, some exhibit the Style in its pathological configuration.

1. Here is a brilliant example. (It won the "Doublespeak" award of the National Council of Teachers of English.)

> The purpose of this project is to develop the capability for institutions of higher learning and community agencies and organizations to coalesce for the development of community services and create a model for the coordination of such services that would maximize the available resources from a number of institutions and provide communication and priority needs and the responses of the educational needs of a given community.

First, translate it into English, if you can. Then point out how it uses the basic elements of the Official Style and to what effect. Finally, try to imagine the social situation which created it. Who wrote it and why?

2. Here is a dialect of The Official Style we have not yet considered, the language of music criticism. How does this dialect differ from the main stream of Official Style. How, for example, does it use nouns, adjectives, and adverbs? General terms? What conception of himself does the reviewer want to project? What conception does he actually project?

> Perhaps it is mere coincidence that Carlos Kleiber chose to record the Beethoven Fifth Symphony, of which his late father, Erich, in 1954 made one of *his* most famous recordings (currently available in England, on Eclipse ECS 518). Still, the comparison is fascinating — and fruitful.
> Perhaps *because* he is his father's son (it is said that Erich discouraged his seeking a career in music),

Carlos necessarily looks for divergent ways of expressing his interpretive ideas, a situation rather analogous to that of Rudolf and Peter Serkin — two great musicians who, for all the obvious differences in repertory sympathies and playing styles, are far more alike in their intense involvement and in their linear pianism than perhaps even they may care to admit!

Both conductors view the symphony's first movement in brisk, fiery terms. They favor a rather terse, impetuous, brightly defined sonority, with stinging accents and sharp articulation taking precedence over the customary "blended" sound of many European orchestras. . . .

In textual terms too the readings are extremely close: In both cases the string/wind antiphony of the coda is rendered with extreme clarity. But whereas Erich tended to eschew rhetorical devices (his is virtually the only recording that allows no extra time whatever for the fermatas in the opening motto), Carlos gives the music more breathing space and, in truth, just avoids mannerism in such strokes as the fractional delays on the chords at bar 58 *et seq.* By going standards, the Carlos Kleiber performance is relatively puristic and light-footed but less clipped and businesslike than his father's. . . .

The *pico rit.* at the beginning of the third movement is a shade overpointed in Carlos Kleiber's reading, but in the main he takes a puristic view. In the celebrated trio for cellos and double basses, he insists on maintaining the tempo. Even Toscanini and Cantelli (obviously no self-indulgent romantics!) let up slightly, as did Erich Kleiber. While the playing is admirably precise, the passage is for me rendered antiseptic compared with all three of those worthy. . . . (Harris Goldsmith, "Carlos Kleiber: Out of the Paternal Shadow," *High Fidelity,* November 1975, p. 91).

3. Here is another example of music criticism, this time
from the rock world. It discusses rock music as "an instrument for the renunciation of the values that had previously enslaved it." This anti-Establishment subject demands an anti-Establishment prose style. The reviewer
tries for a revolutionary directness ("Yes, that was pretty
damned high for anyone to be"), but more often than not
sounds like a sociologist ("simply reshaping your socio-
psychic posture"). And sometimes he falls halfway between sociologese and revolutionary exhortation into a
style we might call the Nonsensical Revolutionary Sublime: "It was the dawning of the upfront electronic head
poem, moving from ecstasy peaks of vision to chilling valleys of alienation from the crunching sterility spawned everywhere." The prose, that is, tries for the colloquial freedom of the low style but is always falling back into the
arms of the Official Style instead. Can you see how The
Official Style threatens to take over a writer and a subject
who want to repudiate everything such a style stands for?
The collision of Officialdom and Revolution seems to combine the hokum of each into things like "the molecular
flow of all possibilities of everyman's collective consciousness." Try translating the passage first into plain English
and then into a low style which really fits the subject. A
really good, gutsy low style is hard to write, isn't it?

 The Philistines would gladly destroy art to make
the world safe once more for sterility, and the question of their success is the issue here. To get high or
not to get high is your own damned business. But the
attempted murder of drug songs would be the act of
socio-cultural warfare whose final implications would
make it everybody's business. The rock outsiders were
constructing alternate approaches to given realities. If
drugs were at times the vehicle or subject, the fact of
some masterpieces still remains.
 The distance between Ben E. King and the Byrds

was a long one in terms of geography, cultural roots and musical perspective on their environment. But the Byrds' fusion of Dylan's material with what was then the unexplored potential of true electric musical freedom was the first large-scale success in deanesthetizing a dead American rock scene. They called it *folk-rock,* and the crystal bridge to acid rock was built by the Byrds themselves.

"Eight miles high . . ."

Yes, that was pretty damned high for anyone to be. What was the air up like there, to haunt someone with the image of Zane Grey towns. *Zane Grey towns* . . . Where were they anyway? Right around the corner America America. It was the dawning of the upfront electronic head poem, moving from ecstasy peaks of vision to chilling valleys of alienation from the crunching sterility sprawled everywhere. The Byrds tumbled through *5D* looking for some answers to the new questions. *"I opened my eyes to the whole universe"* . . . Something exciting was happening in the west. *"I saw the great blunders my teachers had made"* . . .

What happened in the west was probably the most significant creative revolution in the sparse history of American culture. Rock music was evolving itself into an instrument for the renunciation of the values that had previously enslaved it. In the early sixties, Ken Kesey developed the acid notion that you could alter patterns of existence by simply reshaping your socio-psychic posture. Make your "current fantasy" your present reality and just express yourself accordingly. And if the Grateful Dead were propelled by some chemically sent visions in their free-fall haze of "Morning Dew," you could not deny the difference of their music or the fact that the people in the street were listening.

In the west, where the complex beauties of water, woods and canyons raged in contradiction to plastic parking lot vistas and the stuttering of twisted neon, drug songs would emerge as multi-leveled forces molding new conceptions of time and space. " *'Scuse me while I kiss the sky"* . . . The malevolent thundercloud of Hendrix rising from the "Purple Haze," airborne on a guitar that could fly, float or pulverize, would shatter restrictions of musical structure, racial gentility and the intellectual acceptance of defiant obscenity. Hendrix and the Jefferson Airplane were not developing simplistic pro-drug propaganda or tired odes to the joys of getting high. They were artists allowed to "function free," and by expressing the totality of their own experience they would force the blind and tired master critics to admit from the depths of their ignorant souls that there was something of value in those hills. (Richard Gold, "Get Off My Cloud: Drug Music and Artistic Freedom," *Rock,* August 17, 1971, p. 21.)

4. Try translating this summary of a Ph.D. dissertation in literary theory into English. Does it make any sense at all? What kind of impression is it trying to make?

The second part of our study directly confronts mimesis through the examination of those hidden suppressions both implied by and permitting its epistemological foundation. Once sundered from its support in any mythic presence, the literary is seen as both the institution and consummation of man's semiotic adventure as a sign among signs. The individual work is the embodiment of a system of significant *differences,* differences visible only as relationships and never as the derived primacy of a privileged term. It is this action of the difference, as the very manner of its signification, which makes the literary not *something* other than language, but rather that use of language which reveals the structure and potentialities of the sole activity through which man affirms both his freedom and privilege as a sign creature of that signifying universe in which he must dwell.

5. Here is a sample case of The Official Style. What would translating it into English do?

Static budgetary levels of the past several years, coupled with normal incremental costs and inflation, have forced a steady erosion of faculty, staff, trainees and services. These changes have been insidious but have often evolved into significant gaps in core staffing and skewing of programs toward disciplinary or multidisciplinary training rather than the interdisciplinary training on which justification for MCH support is based.

In determining which programs receive supplemental awards, within the above priorities and to the extent funds permit, the degree to which a given program has adhered to the goals and objectives of its approved plan and the overall quality of its training program will be a major consideration.

We are aware that relegation of trainees to a lower level of priority implies that training is of secondary importance. However, such is not the case as training was and is the primary purpose for which our support is intended.

6. Here is a memo from a university president. How would translating it into English weaken its force? How does The Official Style enhance the prestige of the writer? How would you grade this as an example of The Official Style?

As has been planned for some time, these officers will serve under the chairmanship of Dr. Windy as an Administrative Council, advisory to me, providing a new forum for joint review and discussion of all significant academic policy and program issues. In this regard we are particularly fortunate to have on the Council, individuals drawn from each of the Divisions of Letters and Science as well as from the professions. The breadth of background and balance of interests will, it is hoped, provide for ultimate development of coordinated and mutually supportive positions on matters of academic concern.

It is anticipated too that the creation of the Council will provide a more focused mechanism for effective consultation between agencies of the Senate and the Administration. (It is expected that these processes will be further facilitated by assignment of specific responsibility to Vice Chancellor Vague for coordination of Senate-Administration relations.)

Finally it is expected that the Council, representing as it does the full spectrum of the educational program, will provide a more effective administrative interface with individual Departments, Schools, and Colleges in areas falling within its purview. Thus the Council will seek the fullest possible faculty consultation, utilizing both the Senate and departmental structures for determination of faculty views and concerns.

With your cooperation and support, we are convinced that this new administrative structure will prove a positive force for the enhancement of the academic program during the coming years.

7. Here is a very mild example of The Official Style's sociological dialect. Try to get a feeling for its major habits by translating it as briefly as you can (say, five sentences) into English.

THE PROFESSIONAL QUEUER

When demand exceeds supply, it is inevitable that ticket speculators move into the queue in search of supplies for the flourishing market in hard-to-get tickets.

A queue is a line of persons waiting in turn to be served, according to order of arrival. But the act of queue involves more than the acquisition of a right to prior service because of early arrival. To validate this priority, the person must also spend time in the queue, not only to show late-comers that he occupies a given position, but also to demonstrate that his right to priority is confirmed by an unquestionable willingness to undergo further suffering to get the commodity.

. . . The lack of competition for positions among the early-comers can be explained in terms of the reward-cost structure in the first part of the line. In recognition of the conflicting considerations of unnecessary suffering caused by continuous occupancy, and the necessity to validate one's position by spending sometime in residence, various arrangements are made which function to lessen the ordeal while protecting the rights of early-comers. Usually the arrangements represent a compromise which allows the queuer to take brief leaves of absense while retaining undisputed rights of reentry. . . .

First come, first served, the fundamental concept of queuing, is a basic principle of the behavior referred to as distributive justice. . . . There is a direct correspondence between inputs (time spent waiting) and outcomes (preferential service). . . .

In recognition of the fact that continuous residence in the line imposes great hardship, members come to an agreement on the minimum inputs of time necessary to validate occupancy of a position. It is reasonable to claim that rules regulating time spent in

and out of the line are the essential core of the queue
culture.

. . . Keeping close interperson distance also
serves to maintain the "territory" in the face of would-
be intruders. At times of maximum danger . . . there
was a visible bunching together, or shrinkage, in the
physical length of the queue, literally a closing of the
ranks. The exercise of effective social constraints depends on the capacity for cohesive action on the part
of the queuers. At the stadium, whenever outsiders
approached the head of the queue, they were intimi-
dated by vociferous catcalls and jeering. Ordinarily,
this mode of protecting the queue was successful during daylight, the pressure of concerted disapproval
inhibiting all but the boldest. . . .

The culture of the queue also draws upon and in-
corporates elements in a broader culture. The importance of time as a value in Western society is reflected
in the emphasis placed on serving time, and restrictions on time-outs. The way in which people orient
themselves toward a scarce commodity, their preference for cooperation, the entrepreneurial zeal they
display in scalping tickets and charging fees for count-
ing the queue, is a function of broad culture patterns. . . .

In the queue, cohesion is achieved by establishing
informal rules which are kept sufficiently general to
allow individual members to adjust to the normative
pattern.

8. Here are two examples from the psychoanalytic dialect. How do they differ from the sociological passage in
the preceding exercise?

Close inspection will reveal that it is necessary to
infer the operation of several interrelated processes to
account for the outcome which causes one to infer re-

action formation to have been operative. This is another way of saying, of course, that reaction formation does not seem to us to be unitary, elementary or irreducible from a process point of view. Since one outcome of reaction formation is that an instinct derivative is kept unconscious, it can be said that repression is one process operative in reaction formation.

When the integrated part of the mind has been distorted in a bygone period by an unusual splitting off of those aspects of established functions which precipitated experiences of overwhelming disorganization or unpleasure as they were being increasingly utilized by normally emerging instinctual drive representatives, then the split-off portion can be regarded as a surviving representative of instinctual operations responsible for the formation or the maintenance of phase-specific mental organization.

CHAPTER SIX

The School Style

So the errors we've been examining don't occur at random. They fall into a pattern. The rhythmless, shapeless, verbless, and often mindless word bags constitute an act of stylistic imitation. Students have developed their own version of The Official Style. We might call it The School Style. The School Style reaches the student more by example and osmosis than by direct teaching, but it is not less effectively taught for that reason. School is a bureaucracy and a bureaucracy requires some version of The Official Style. And, as with The Official Style, the impulses leading students to write The School Style do not all stem from laziness or villainous conspiracy. The desire to do what is expected plays its part, too. Like the parent Official Style, The School Style reflects the circumstances that have called it forth. What is it like?

Well, in summary, it is compounded, in equal parts, of deference to a teacher of supposedly traditional tastes, of despair at filling up the required number of pages before tomorrow morning, and of the mindlessness born of knowing that what you write may not be read with real attention. Above all, The School Style avoids unqualified assertion. It always leaves the back door open. If the teacher doesn't agree, you can sneak out through an "it seems" for "is," "may indeed have something in common with" for "results from," "it could possibly be argued that" for

"I think," and so on. Rule 2 requires that you fill up the page as quickly as possible. Never "feel isolated"; always "suffer from an acute feeling of isolation." Never "feel alienated"; always "feel like an outsider, alienated from the society of 'normal' men." This desire to fill up the page works whenever we write from demand and not desire, of course, but it works insidiously, even when you are not deliberately trying to fill the page with bullshit. It constitutes the major barrier to student revision: "I've finally managed to squeeze out five pages and now you want to *cut it down*? If I cut it down to two, what else can I find to say? And will it be all right if, like, I just 'say it'? Will I get credit for that?" It's The Official Style all over again.

If you want to make plain sense, then you've got to cut and go back to the drafting board for fresh ideas. If you want to write hokum, or if only hokum will impress, then hokum is your play. In school as outside it, more often than not hokum works. But if you want to make reasonable sense, you'll have to leave The School Style behind. It has all the bad elements of The Official Style but none of its sublime stiffness, none of its fun. You don't want to write slang either, but something in between. That middle ground, in fact, that we saw evaporating in favor of The Official Style on the one hand and spastic "you-know" conversation on the other. This kind of middle style aims above all at authority, at convincing your reader that you have a right to speak, are the kind of person who is *likely* to have something to say. To do this, you must seem in control of both language and its social context.

First, controlling language. What matters first is insignificant detail. Spelling mistakes, typos, mistakes in idiom, unfashionable usages, all these characterize you as a writer controlled by language rather than controlling it. You present yourself as still in rompers. It is not a question of being *clear*. These revelations of self don't usually obscure ideas: they obscure you. Worse, they reveal you. They reveal that you have not paid attention to your own writing and invite the reader to respond in kind. They model the history of your mind. Take errors in idiomatic prepositions, for example. They have started cropping up significantly only in the last dozen years. They speak volumes. They are the kind of mistakes foreigners make when learning English. They are conventions you learn by heart when you learn the language. If you have grown up speaking English and still use unidiomatic prepositions, you've declared to your reader your ignorance of the body of written English that has established these idioms. A linguist would argue, of course, that you've simply illustrated that idiom is a changing thing. Of course. But you don't want, even so, to make this declaration of ignorance. You don't want to confess that you've bypassed your written culture. Or if you do, you'll want at least to know that you are doing so.

We are talking about the eloquence of seemingly inconsequential detail. I read "the proximity of liquor stores *from* campuses" and believe no further. If the writer does not know that things are "proximate *to*," then he is blind in a hundred other suspect ways. Or I read this:

> Many (though not all) students of animal neurosis have been preoccupied in producing syndromes resembling those found in human neurosis, rather than in determining the precise way in which symptoms arise.

"Preoccupied in" rather than "preoccupied *with*" loses the reader's confidence out of all proportion to the offense. Perhaps it ought not be this way, but it is. We make, after all, such judgments in life every day. We distrust someone because, well, there is just something about him, about how he dresses or smiles or talks. He may be as honest as the day is long but we won't buy a used car from him. We continually make large judgments from small stylistic clues. When a writer mates a singular subject with a plural verb, we wonder if he can count to two. When he cannot form the possessive case correctly, tell "it's" from "its" for example, or "pool's" from "pools," we wonder the same thing. A professor sets as rubric for an examination question, "You are Becket. You have been assigned to cover the crucifiction of Christ by a national magazine," and we reply, "Well, if by a national magazine, it would be a cruci-*fiction*," and the professor never recovers.

Authority in prose is not entirely, or even primarily, a logical affair. It depends, in a negative way, on observing conventions, as we've just seen. Observing a society's conventions proves that you've been trained in them and are thus a member of that society. And *this is the first thing the reader wants to know.* Societies vary, obviously. You'll hold out one kind of stylistic assurance, observe one set of conventions, in writing for the *New York Times* and another in writing for the *L. A. Free Press.* You never use a four-letter word for the first, scarcely anything else for the second, but the same rule prevails for both. You've got to *show,* without *declaring,* your right to speak. Just *saying* "Listen to me" will get you nowhere. You've got to show — awful as this sounds in a democracy — that you've been properly brought up. There are shortcuts, not only dictionaries but usage dictionaries and manuals of all kinds, Emily Post books for language. They help, but they are no substitute for the real thing. If you want to write well, you've got to read widely and with attention. It is just like life. If you don't pay attention, you'll give yourself away. The small mistakes are often the largest.

Here is an example of just this self-betrayal. A student-bureaucrat tries to defend herself, prove herself worthy of trust, and does just the opposite. The article is called, mindlessly enough, "Does she or doesn't she?"

My recent election to the vice presidency of the National Student Association has surfaced much criticism and confusion from both the *Daily Blast* and the Student Legislative Council. Resultingly, the *Blast* in its . . . editorial summarized such a train of events as "ever-thickening smoke here at Old Frothingslosh.

I would like to clear up these smoke-filled thoughts that have focused from my attendance at the 27th National Student Congress in St. Louis. At the final SLC meeting, the majority granted me full delegate privileges.

As attested to in your article, the definition of "observer" must be questioned. Agreeing wholeheartedly, once affiliation . . . was approved, my Congress status changed from that of a non-member observer to a delegate. The rights accorded to this newly obtained position included full-speaking privileges, participation in and with such internal, Congress overseers as the Congress Steering Committee, and the ability to run for office. Council was not deceived as to the intentions for seeking the retroactive affiliation: in fact, it was agreed that I would see what NSA "was really like."

In fulfilling such an obligation, I viewed the Congress as a finished product — what the delegates buy — and as a structure in its formulation stages. Serving with the Congress Steering Committee afforded Old Frothingslosh both an external and an internal evaluation . . . the latter often neglected, yet just as critical to an organization's success.

Fortunately, the "convention politics" your editorial refers to did not catch my glimpse until Thursday evening 24 hours prior to the balloting. Having declined the nomination on Wednesday (knowing not from whence it came), I had to garner the unanimous consent of the assembled delegates to run. Furthermore, I lost the vast amount of publicity given declared candidates in Thursday's and Friday's Congress News. The final publication was to include platforms and thus had a deadline of 7:30 P.M., Thursday. . . .

Tuned in with their disenchantment, was a public censuring of my actions — not my election, but rather certain statements termed, by them, as unnecessary, disrespectful, and improper. Although I viewed that section of the report as a critical update, or at least an opportunity to put in writing what I personally have confronted in the NSA battle since taking office in June, I must admit that I have refreshed Council's memory a little bit too much. However, I still doubt the attention span of students that are surrounded by a labyrinth of issues: that definitely includes me. . . .

What kind of mind is revealed here? Clearly one operating at the limits of adhesion. A number of problems strike the eye, but look for a moment only at the elementary errors in grammar, syntax, and idiom:

"has surfaced much criticism"
> You cannot use "surface" as a transitive verb (one that takes a direct object) in English. A porpoise can "surface" or you can bring it to the surface in a net, but you cannot "surface" it.

"to clear-up these smoke-filled thoughts that have focused from my attendance"
> You can focus "on" something but not "from" it. Nor can you "focus" a smoke-filled thought. Presumably the writer means that the thoughts have *come into focus because of* the attendance.

"As attested to in your article"
> "Attest" is not a synonym for "mention" or "argue."

"Agreeing wholeheartedly"
> This participial phrase, as written, modifies "my Congress status" not, as presumably it is meant to, the writer.

"full-speaking"
> A hyphen is used in compounds when used adjectivally, as in Homer's "rosy-fingered dawn." Here "full" is simply an adverb modifying "speaking" and so no hyphen is needed.

"internal, Congress"
> No comma needed or possible here.

"Council was not deceived"
> Idiomatic English: "The Council."

"did not catch my glimpse"
> No such idiom in English. "I glimpsed" or "catch my eye."

"from whence"
> "Whence" means "from where."

"garner the unanimous consent"
> "Garner" means to store, hoard up, and hence makes no sense here.

"tuned in with their disenchantment, was"
> "Tuned in" simply makes no sense here as a synonym for "agree."

"However, I still doubt the attention span of students that are surrounded by a labyrinth of issues: that definitely includes me."
> To "doubt the attention span" of someone makes no sense. You can doubt that it is long — or short — or, if you say so, that it exists at all. But you cannot simply "doubt" it anymore than you can "doubt" the World Trade Center. The relative pronoun used to refer to people ("students")

is "who," not "that." A relative pronoun must, of course, refer back to a specific noun, not, as with the second "that," to an entire preceding thought.

Even such a preliminary list of problems suggests that the smoke she talks about will remain ever-thickening. But the real damage comes not in the reporting but in the presentation of self. Here is someone who has not learned the elementary rules of the language, who is continually imprisoned by media clichés ("critical update," "tuned in"), who time and again simply does not know what words mean ("prospects" for office cannot mar an attendance record), who uses gobbets of The Official Style ("as a structure in its foundation stages") without understanding what, if anything, they might mean. The prose reveals a mind that thinks entirely in half-understood, half-digested, half-grammatical fragments. That such a person could hold high student office in a major university, that nobody should even *notice* this kind of prose, suggests that, in the university, too, The Official Style rules. Hokum works. She got elected.

But most of us don't want to write this way. We don't want to bullet-proof our argument by imitating The Official Style. Everyone says, "Be yourself," but the prose writer should always want to do a little better than this, seem more in control than, when he first took pen in hand, he really was. Writing gains its power from the condensed effort revision permits. When we read a passage, we instinctually assume that the writer spent an equivalent time writing it, instead of ten times as long. From that sleight-of-hand condensation comes prose's power, its authority. Ideally, then, all the techniques of revision we've considered thus far ought to strengthen the authority of prose.

Let's look at a few passages with this in mind. Careful revision can often bring a dramatic increase in authority. Here are the first and second drafts of a student paper's opening paragraph. The second was submitted after the first had been marked up according to the Paramedic Method.

ORIGINAL

Since *Venus and Adonis* is a narrative poem about courtship, its reader might reasonably expect the work to depict, at some point, the lover wooing, persuading the beloved. And indeed we do find Venus wooing Adonis through most of the work . . . unsuccessfully. But as much as a poem can be said to be "about" one topic or another, the number of lines given to Venus' effort and the fact that the courtship fails might therefore indicate that this poem may very well be more "about" persuasion than courtship, "about" Venus' failure — to be more specific — to operate in a rhetorical mode which will finally appeal to Adonis. Immediately preceding his departure, in one of his longest speeches in the poem, Adonis tells Venus why she has failed to woo him: "I hate not love," he says, "but your device in love." According to Neilson and Hill, the young man's words refer to the goddess' behavior; yet this clause couched as it is within a speech dealing with language, a speech which shows Adonis critical of an over-handled theme, wary of the speaker's treatise, armed against the sound of her tongue's tune, hateful of her device, scornful of her indiscriminate vocabulary, offended by her wanton talk and feeling himself an "orator too green" to debate her successfully (770–806), this speech carries further implications which consequently add to Adonis' protests a rhetorical aspect.

REVISION

A narrative poem about courtship, *Venus and Adonis* might lead a reader to expect a portrayal of the lover wooing the beloved. Instead, we find Venus wooing Adonis unsuccessfully. The number of lines, therefore, given to Venus' failing effort indicate that this poem may be "about" persuasion more than courtship: Venus finally cannot speak Adonis' language. Just before leaving, in one of his longest speeches, Adonis tells Venus why she failed: "I hate not love," he says, "but your *device* in love." What does he mean by device? Perhaps he means her behavior. Yet the rest of his speech concerns language. Adonis criticizes Venus' overhandled theme, and protects himself against her pleas. When she speaks, he finds her careless choice of words and bawdy language offensive. Adonis feels himself, finally, an orator "too green" to debate her successfully (770–806). Thus his entire speech protests against her rhetoric.

Lots of improvements here, especially in the rhythm. That dreadful last sentence, for example, shapeless and hopelessly repetitive, has been excised. But notice especially how the revision aims not to explain too much. The original offers its points in the typical academic way, exhaustively: "*reasonably* expect," "at some point," "wooing" and "persuading," "through most of the work" and so on. And it weasels so: "might reasonably expect," "as much as a poem can be said to be about one topic or another," "might therefore indicate." Nail every point to the floor but still leave the back door open just in case. Nobody believes prose like this. Start out with an opening paragraph like the original one and the reader, if he has a choice, reads no further.

The revision has tried, as well, to lower the *level* of the original. The original is written in The School Style. You can see it in just one phrase: "Immediately preceding his departure." No one would say this in ordinary conversation. You'd say, "just before leaving." And the paper should say it too. Don't imitate the looseness of speech but keep your prose close to its idioms. Don't commence.

Begin. Don't talk about an "individual." Talk about a "person." Let your thinking and your controlled prose tell the reader you're worth listening to. Don't translate everything into The Student Style. And don't open with trumpets, as here:

> William Shakespeare undoubtedly drank from the waters of the fountain of Parnassus, first, before he began his narrative poem, *Venus and Adonis,* and again before he worked into that poem two digressions — one describing Adonis's "trampling courser," and the other describing a hare's race from the hunting hounds. Both digressions contrast the character of Adonis with the individual likenesses of the two animals.

Cut out all this silly guff. Just begin. And unless you're writing at length — more than five pages, say — don't close with trumpets either. Just stop.

Once you've chosen a level, formal or informal, stick to it. Don't, as in this example, start out colloquially only to sink by degrees into The School Style:

> The anthropology vogue is sure to peak eventually, even if only when meddling ethnologists have unwittingly made everyone everywhere just like us — and when it does, linguistics will surely be where it's at. Extricated from some of its bafflingly esoteric complexities, transformational grammar is the heady stuff of which academic fads are made. Already anyone with access to John Lyon's cute little *haute vulgarisation* of Chomsky in the modish series of Fontana Modern Masters paperbacks can easily appear as one of the gnostic. Soon, sandwiched between Sani-Flush ads, young Noam — a Kantian-rationalist-anarchist-philosopher and occasional linguist who can match

McLuhan eclecticism for catchy eclectism — will trade quips with Dick Cavett. B. F. Skinner will demand equal-time. I can see it all now.

Until then, while it is still not utterly naive to speak of the Chomsky-Fodor-Katz-Postal philosophies of mind and language as scientific theories and not as cult ideologies, we can cull some very significant insights into certain problems in philosophy, psychology, and social science from the "Chomsky revolution" and its infrastructure, structuralism. But the urge to publicize remains, for among the giants of structuralism — Claude Levi-Strauss and Jean Piaget being the others — Chomsky is alone in realizing the truly frightening political and social implications of, and in intuiting the power of structuralism as a radical antidote to, positivism and scientism. Chomsky's self-styled rationalism is one of the few credible defenses against creeping behaviorism and cultural relativism, against Hebbian accounts of consciousness, against the increasingly powerful notion that man is nothing more than a genetically and socially programmed machine, and against the Brave New World of operant conditioning, behavior modification, and cultural engineering that is already upon us.

What a last sentence! The indignation we are supposed to feel disappears beneath a terminological landslide of "creeping behaviorism," "cultural relativism," "operant conditioning," "behavior modification," and "cultural engineering." We are drowned in "-isms" and "-shuns," each with its own adjective. No one can keep straight such a torrent of terms. The writer trips over his own tone. Tone is usually defined as the implied relationship of reader and writer. This means that it involves a presentation of self.

What kind of person wrote this irate letter to the editor?

In response to the November 18 article in the *Daily Blast* entitled "Dental Student charges bias" and the *Blast* editorial, one must consider the following salient point before a final denouement can be attained. Mr. Jones purports that he was a victim of discrimination, nevertheless, was he in fact passing all of his courses at the time of his dismissal? This matter is imperative in order to draw a meaningful conclusion to this acute problem.

You notice first the errors in idiom. You don't "attain" a "denouement"; "purports" usually carries a complementary infinitive ("purports to be"); you don't draw a conclusion "to" a problem. And how explain what is wrong with that last sentence? Like the rest of the passage, it seems glued together from fragments, predigested phrases borrowed from The Official Style: "this matter," "it is imperative that," "meaningful conclusion," "acute problem." But the parts don't fit. They carry, in fact, The Official Style to its impersonal extreme — there are no people at all in the sentence, only possible bureaucratic responses.

We see here the difference between mistakes coming from plain ignorance — the old-fashioned "This is the reason I came to college to learn how to become a football coach" type — and The School Style kind. The School Style comes not from faulty speech patterns but from a misguided act of stylistic imitation. It creates a prose very like that written by a foreigner just learning English. Written in ordinary English, the letter might have read:

The 18 November article, "Dental student charges bias" fails to mention a crucial point: was Mr. Jones passing all his courses when he was dismissed?

We'll never know whether the writer could have written such a letter or not. Clearly, though, the verbal world he lived in urged him to do otherwise, to try to write in a language he only partly understood. The result is the beginner's version of The Official Style — The School Style.

It appears in many guises. Look, for example, at this nearly incoherent student paper. The subject, sex, almost vanishes behind the bureauratic language.

> Shakespeare took a natural phenomenon and incorporated it into the poem at such a time and place and in such a style to make several appropriate statements, in his first digression. Lust, as experienced by the two horses, proves unashamed, uncontrolled, and it is expressed without reluctance brought about by the workings of the conscience. These are not only the manifestations of lust in nature, according to the poet, but the wish fulfillment of Venus. Venus experiences similar physical vigor from lust and she performs like manners of wooing to those experienced and performed by the male horse. Both use the uncontrolled power of their lust to set themselves up with their match. Venus snatches Adonis from his horse, so too, the horse crushed the bit between his teeth. In a more subdued manner, he employs controlled gestures specifically with his love in mind, that reveal all his intents to her. Such gestures compare to Venus' urging poetry and luring gestures used to woo Adonis. Venus would wish that Adonis respond to her approaches. The jennet, in a courtly manner, feigns disdain of male lust to make herself a more attractive prize. She momentarily controls her lust, soon, voluntarily to resign to it.

How has The Official Style served as a model here? You can almost see it governing the nascent thought. The "natural phenomenon" is animal sexuality, but sexuality is specific and concrete; instead we are given it at the highest level of impersonal generality — "a natural phenomenon." The doubling of the verb ("took" and "incorporated") finds a legalistic echo in "at such a time and place and in such a style," and in the bloodless neutrality of "to make several appropriate statements." The sexual excitement and the comedy simply evaporate into thin air. A writer less sterilized by The Official Style might have written "In the first digression, the stallion and the mare can finally get it together, albeit in epic terms, but Venus and Adonis cannot." Notice how, in the second sentence of the passage, the action (the sexual desire) is taken away from the natural subject (the horses who feel it) and displaced into a noun — and a human noun at that — "lust"? The passage includes a good deal of pure lard, too: "expressed without reluctance brought about by the workings of the conscience," passed through the PM, comes out "expressed without remorse" and since this means the same thing as "proves unashamed" it can be removed altogether. The PM works just as well on the next two sentences. Look at them:

> These are not only the manifestations of lust in nature, according to the poet, but the wish fulfillment of Venus. Venus experiences similar physical vigor from lust and she performs like manners of wooing to those experienced and performed by the male horse.

This is not incorrect prose. It is pathological prose, sick with bureaucratic constipation, a special language suitable for schools but not for sensible human life. In ordinary speech, this wordy guff boils down to "Venus, too, is hot to trot." This is, of course, too lively for school, but even "Venus, too, lusts after a mate" would be better.

The School Style will go to any length to kill and bury the action: "Both use the uncontrolled power of their lust to set themselves up with their match." As written, the sentence makes no sense at all, but down there somewhere lurks a root assertion for this sentence and the next. It goes something like: "Both attack directly; Venus snatches Adonis from his horse, the horse crushes his bit between his teeth and gallops off to cover the mare."

The School Style prose is not written by chance or from laziness. You have to work at it. People have to be taught to write this way. Prose like this is the standard dialect of a bureaucratic society. Although it may include errors of grammar and syntax, it is not basically *incorrect;* it poses a different problem altogether. If you write this way, it is because you are rehearsing for writing The Official Style. That is the main purpose of a passage such as we've just examined. That the passage is largely incomprehensible does not, in this context, really matter. If it lacks significance, it lacks significance in the right way; if vacuous and long-winded, it is so in the approved fashion. Such a passage bears eloquent witness to style as our final, if often subconscious, act of allegiance.

Here is a final example of The Official Style's influence. The passage comes from a paper submitted in an upper-division English class at a major university by an upper-middle-class student. Lots of things have gone wrong here, obviously, but can you see the influence of The Official Style seeping up through the incoherence?

> Politics; strategins of power, are these the means to entreat a lover, or are they the means by which one looses the goal? I say the later. For as will be showen, by these means Venus lost Adonis.
>
> "Man is by nature a political animal." In this quote Aristotle was not speaking of the political ways of man or woman, the animal, to ensnare, but of the political ways people socialize and conform. Politic, like many words, has many meanings. Today in an election year we hear the word often and see it used by our presidential candidates in actions to illisit other actions to achieve ones goal. These actions, these political manouvers bloom in power, threts, seductions, force, temptations, insults, flatories, mockery, and devious

appeals. Through time, man has remained loyal to these means, for the ploys we see used today in Carter-Ford debate, are the same as Shakespear used to have Venus snare a mate.

Power, how lustfilled you can be. What beautifly invisioned goals you have the means to obtain. How treacherous may be your ways, and yet, the victor you not always can be. How do you conquor indifference? Can you always squelsh resistance? Is love within your relm or is lust your sole desire?

Power is a force often used through pressure to influence. Pressure when applied subordinates the pressed and often does not impress; rather, breeds ambivilance, resistance, and antagonism. This we see in "Venus and Adonis." The pressor the influenceor the power, is Venus. The resistance comes from Adonis, no matter how much Venus applies insistance.

Venus' means to obtain her goal — the love of Adonis, are exactly what blows it for her to be the victor. She uses power, pressure, coercion — politicing, in order to win love. She does not perceive that her means anihilate acts of cooperation and resiprosity — nessesary factors for love. In other words, her means anihilate her goal.

Such prose projects a genuine if pathetic eloquence. The writer hungers after a rhythm she doesn't begin to know how to create. Look at the gesture toward climax in "The pressor the influenceor the power, is Venus," or the try for balance in "Is love within your relm or is lust your sole desire?" Once or twice the style really scores, as when it nails to the wall a central identity, sex and power: "Power, how lustfilled you can be." More often, though, this hunger for a prose with some life falls back into The Official Style: "She does not perceive that her means anihilate acts of cooperation and resiprosity — necessary factors for love."

Sad, isn't it? Way down there lurks a gift for words, and yet it can find expression only in media cliché ("Today in an election year we hear"), in Official Style jargon ("influencor" — like, I suppose, the influencee), and in spelling so bad that it must represent a subconscious loathing for the printed page. If you want to love words, and are offered nothing but The Official Style, maybe this — in an extreme case — is where you end up. Such prose makes us see not only how omnipresent The Official Style is, but how absent any other prose role models really are in American society today. If you want to make love to words, play games of balance and accumulation and sound with them, you don't have any place to go. Again, The School Style doesn't happen to you by accident. The smaller bureaucracy is rehearsing you for the larger one.

Now, two dramatic before-and-after improvements, using our PM. Try to describe why the revisions seem more mature, more authoritative, less like school exercises. This is not easy to do. Both examples show how elusive authority is in prose, and yet how closely related to small changes in rhythm, shape, and emphasis. In each case, the revision manages to excise that written-to-fulfill-an-assignment tone that haunts student prose and becomes so important a part of The Official Style later on.

1. BEFORE

In comparing the various seventeenth and eighteenth-century writings and rewritings of *The Tempest* (Shakespeare–1611; Dryden-Davenant–1667; Shadwell–1674; Purcell's resetting of Shadwell–1695; Garrick–1756) among the most significant things to be observed are the changes in the style, function and amount of music in the productions. From a musical standpoint these changes readily fall into a pattern which can be traced within the context of the emergence of English opera. With each play the music became a more dominant element, and consideration of this fact is necessary to an understanding of changes in the respective texts of the plays. Drama was becoming music-drama. Not only the tone and style, but the very fabric of the play was altered significantly as Dryden and Davenant, Shadwell, and Purcell became involved in creating a different kind of theatre, a different kind of entertainment from that which Shakespeare had produced. The importance of understanding this cannot be overestimated. It is essential to understanding why and how these plays were realized as they were and how they are to be compared to one another. In this paper different versions of the song "Full Fathom Five" will be compared for the purpose of tracing and analyzing the musical changes to be found. Understanding the kinds of changes brought about in the music provides an important perspective from which to understand the natures of the different plays.

AFTER

Restoration audiences experienced a drama strikingly different from that their Jacobean grandparents applauded 60 years earlier. By 1700, English theatre had been transformed as Dryden and his contemporaries reshaped the tradition they inherited. The way Restoration playwrights and composers changed theatre music reflects the way they transformed theatre itself. Not only did they use more music than their predecessors, they used music of a different kind differently. Musical changes mirror other changes. "Full Fathom Five's" musical transformation from production to production illustrates a changing sensibility.

2. BEFORE

T. S. Eliot's "Preludes" first appeared in Wyndham Lewis's experimental periodical of "the Great English Vortex." *Blast* was to have been the voice of the modern art of England, and contained contributions of Lewis, Ford Madox Ford, Ezra Pound, Gaudier-Brzeska, and in the second and final number of July, 1915, "Preludes" and "Rhapsody of a Windy Night" by T. S. Eliot. The magazine was filled with artistic polemic and social iconoclasm; *Blast* proposed to reform the stale art of Decadence and Impressionism, to convert the King to Vorticism, to unleash artistic energy, and to produce a classless art of the individual of Northern Europe.

Such a journal seems an unlikely place for an author such as Eliot, writing poems such as the "Preludes," to publish his work. Instead of vigorous energy, they project urban languour and a self-conscious author. As has been demonstrated from the original manuscript, the "Preludes" do in fact deal with the anonymous urban poor; the poems were originally titled by the South Boston neighborhoods of Dorchester and Roxbury. The third "Prelude" originally carried an epigraph, referring to a "petite putain," from a low-life French novel, *Bubu de Montparnasse*. The stanzas of the "Preludes" show no trace of the vehemence of one of Pound's contributions to *Blast*.

AFTER

T. S. Eliot's "Preludes" first appeared in Wyndham Lewis's experimental periodical, *Blast,* which printed contributions from a close circle representing the Modernist movement, including Ford Madox Ford, Ezra Pound, and Henri Gaudier-Brzeska. *Blast* nearly choked on its artistic polemic and social iconoclasm: it threatened to reform stale Decadence and Impressionism, convert King George V to Vorticism, and unleash an individual, classless art representative of Northern European energy. World War I killed *Blast,* but not before the second, final issue of July 1915 unhesitatingly offered "Preludes" and "Rhapsody of a Windy Night" to a distracted world.

Blast's splenetic pages seem an unlikely vehicle for urban languor and timorous self-consciousness. Instead of vigorous energy, "Preludes" withdraw to the anonymous urban poor; they originally carried the titles "Dorchester" and "Roxbury," South Boston slums, and the third section bore an epigraph from a low-life French novel, *Bubu de Montparnasse.* Their quiescence stands at the furthest extreme from Pound's vehemence.

Here are some shorter and more extreme examples of The School Style for practice. Once again, as a reminder, the Paramedic Method:

1. Circle the prepositions.
2. Circle the "is" forms.
3. Ask "Who is kicking who?"
4. Put this "kicking" action in a simple (not compound) active verb.
5. Start fast — no mindless introductions.
6. Write out each sentence on a blank sheet of paper and mark off its basic rhythmic units.
7. Mark off sentence lengths.
8. Read the passage aloud with emphasis and feeling.

Translating into plain English is only the first step. The translating may reduce a paragraph to a phrase or to the native nothingness whence it came. Ask, in each case, how The School Style has cast its malign shadow. Can you see, from time to time (e.g., in "sharer of his solitude, but also the sacker of his solitude") a hunger for verbal play The School Style cannot feed?

1. Behavior, words and body movements are gestures that evoke similar, identical and unique responses or reactions to the individual or community initiating the gesture. Paradoxically, gestures which create immediate perceptions, may direct or misdirect the person or community trying to interpret the motivation or meaning behind those gestures.

2. Bearing this definition in mind, it is possible to speak of these four selections as four prose descriptions: We have descriptions of a social system, a night, a village and a fight. Each author approaches his description with a different style and emphasis.

3. If we noted that Parsons' prose is polysyllabic, then we must also note that Virginia Woolf's prose is monosyllabic.

4. This short sentence's image reflects the rising and falling of the sea, while the thought that the image expresses supports the thought of the selections: that the extent of a man's soul must expand to encompass not only the sharer of his solitude, but also the sacker of his solitude.

5. In this piece of literature, words and images are so littered that their importance as units is subordinated to the unity of the prose description.

6. It is always a joy to read an excellent piece of literature, sometimes primarily because of the ideas contained in the piece, but more often because of the manner in which the ideas are presented — the style of the piece. This is the case with Francis Bacon's essay "On Friendship."

7. "London." This sentence is somewhat brief. Yet, the one word, London, succeeds in informing the reader that the meat of this paragraph concerns London.

8. And because clichés are clichés because they are so overused they are exemplary of how language is developing not into a viable means of communication but simply a repetition of trite platitudes uttered at appropriate moments.

9. The essay revealed the author's understanding of idea presentation. He supported each idea with historical references and then he added his personal support to the idea stated. He included references to the universe, the heaven, the galaxy, and religion in his presentation.

CHAPTER SEVEN

Why Bother?

I've been arguing that much of the prose problem comes from the cluster of goals and attributes that make up The Official Style. To this degree the paramedic analogy holds and the prose can be revised using simple procedures. We have seen what The Official Style looks like: dominantly a noun style; a concept style; a style whose sentences have no design, no shape, rhythm, or emphasis; an unreadable, voiceless, impersonal style; a style built on euphemism and various kinds of poetic diction; a style with a formulaic structure, "is" plus a string of prepositional phrases before and after. And we've seen how to revise it. A set of do-it-yourself techniques, the Paramedic Method, handles the problem nicely.

But you may well be asking, at this point, why bother? Why try to see in a blind world? There are two answers, or rather two kinds of answers. The first kind: "If you can see and others can't, you'll get ahead." Sometimes this is true and sometimes not. Generally, it helps to write better prose. It makes for a better statement of purpose when you apply for law school or a job. It will probably not, however, get you a better grade on a sociology paper, where plain prose sounds simple-minded or even flip. The sensible procedure here: learn both languages, the plain and The Official Style. The second kind of answer is both simpler than the first and more complex. We've looked at many examples of inept student writing — writing that ranges from shapeless to mindless. The second kind of answer to "Why bother?" is simply, "Are you willing to sign your name to what you have written? To present yourself in public — whether it matters to anyone else or not — as this kind of person?" In a sense, it is a simple question: "Whatever the advantage — or disadvantage — ought I do this?" The primary kind of moral question: If everyone else is committing murder, ought I do the same? Do you choose to encounter the world on its terms or on your own? A simple question but one we must all answer for ourselves. "The style is the man," people often say. Perhaps they mean that to this basic moral question you'll give the same answer for writing as for the rest of your behavior. Yet the question is complex, too, for what kind of behavior is "prose behavior"? Prose is usually described in a moral vocabulary — "sincere," "open" or "devious," and "hypocritical" — but is this vocabulary justified? Why, for that matter, has it been so moralistic? Why do so many people feel that bad prose threatens the foundations of civilization? And why, in fact, do we think "bad" the right word to use for it?

Let's start with the primary ground for morality, the self. We may think of the self as both a dynamic and a static entity. It is static when we think of ourselves as having central, fixed selves independent of our surroundings, an "I" we can remove from society without damage, a central self inside our head. But it becomes dynamic when we think of ourselves as actors playing social roles, a series of roles which vary with the social situation in which we find ourselves. Such a social self amounts to the sum of all the public roles we play. Our complex identity comes from the constant interplay of these two kinds of self. Our final identity is usually a mixed one, few of us being completely the same in all situations or, conversely, social chameleons who change with every context. What allows the self to grow and develop is the free interplay between these two kinds of self. If we were completely sincere we would always say exactly what we think — and cause social chaos. If we were always acting an appropriate role, we would be certifiably insane. Reality, for each of us, presents itself as constant oscillation between these two extremes.

When we say that writing is sincere, we mean that somehow it has managed to express this complex oscillation, this complex self. It has caught the accent of a particular self, a particular mixture of the two selves. Sincerity can't point to any *specific* verbal configuration, of course, since sincerity varies as widely as man himself. The sincere writer has not said exactly what he felt in the first words that occur to him. That might produce a revolutionary tirade, or "like-you know" conversational babble, or the gross student mistakes we've been reviewing. Nor has a sincere writer simply borrowed a fixed language, as when a bureaucrat writes in The Official Style. He has managed to create a style which, like the social self, can become part of society, can work harmoniously in society and, at the same time, like the central self, can represent his unique selfhood. He holds his two selves in balance; this is what "authority" in prose really means.

Now simply reverse this process. What the act of writing prose involves for the writer is an integration of his self, a deliberate act of balancing its two component parts. It represents an act of socialization, and it is by repeated acts of such socialization that we become sociable beings, that we grow up. Thus, the act of writing models the presentation of self in society, constitues a rehearsal for social reality. It is not simply a question of a preexistent self making its message known to a preexistent society. It is not, initially, a question of message at all. Writing is a way to clarify, strengthen, and energize the self, to render individuality rich, full, and social. This does not mean writing that flows, as Terry Southern immortally put it, "right out of the old guts onto the goddam paper." Just the opposite. Only by taking the position of the reader toward one's own prose, putting a reader's pressure on it, can the self be made to grow. Writing should enhance and expand the self, allow it to try out new possibilities, tentative selves.

The moral ingredient in writing, then, works first not on the morality of the message but on the nature of the sender, on the complexity of the self. "Why bother?" To invigorate and enrich your selfhood, to increase, in the most literal sense, your self-consciousness. Writing, properly pursued, does not make you better. It makes you more alive. This is why our growing illiteracy ought to distress us. It tells us something, something alarming, about the impoverishment of our selves. We say that we fear written communication will break down. Unlikely. And if it does we can always, as we do anyway, pick up the phone. Something more fundamental is at stake, the self-hood and sociability of the communicators. We are back to the basic peculiarity of *writing* — it is *premeditated* utterance, and in that premeditation lives its first if not its only value. "Why bother?" "To find out who I really am." It is not only what we think that we discover in writing, but what we are and can be.

We can now see why the purely neutral, transparent style is so hard to write and so rare, and why we take to jargon, to The Official Style, to all the varieties of poetic diction, verbal ornament, with such alacrity. We are doing more in writing, any writing, than transmitting neutral messages. We want to convey our feelings about what we say, our attitude toward the human relationships we are thus establishing. Neutral communications do not come naturally to man. What matters most to him is his relationships with his fellow men. These urges continually express themselves through what we write. They energize what we call style. Style has attracted a moralistic vocabulary because it expresses all the patterns of human behavior which morality must control. This moralistic vocabulary leads to a good deal of confusion, but it arises naturally enough from the way human beings use literary style.

How rare a purely neutral human relationship really is you can see simply by reflecting on your daily life. Is there any response, however trivial, that we don't color with hand gestures, facial expressions, postures of the body? Human beings are nonstop expressors, often through minute subconscious clues. We sense, immediately, that a friend is angry at us by the way he says "Hello." He doesn't say, "Go to hell, you skunk" instead of "Hello." He doesn't need to. Tense vocal chords, pursed lips, a curt bob of the head perhaps, do just as well. No one has put a percentage figure to this kind of human communication, but it far outranks plain statement in frequency and importance. The same truth prevails for written communication. We are always trying to say more than we actually do. This voice-over technique is our natural way of speaking.

We can now begin to see what kinds of value judgments make sense about prose and what kind don't. The prevailing wisdom teaches that the best prose style is the most transparent, the least seen; prose ideally aspires to a perfect neutrality; like the Perfect Secretary, it gets the job done without intruding. Rare we have seen this ideal to be. But is it even ideal? Doesn't it rule out most of what we call good prose? The ideal document of perfect neutrality would be a laundry list. We mean by good prose something a little different. We mean a style suffused with a sense of human relationships, of specific occasions and why they matter. We mean a style which expresses a genuinely complex and fully socialized self. We've cleared up a lot of muddy student writing up to now. The metaphor "clear up" is clear enough, and there is no reason not to use it, but we can now explain more precisely what we have been doing. An incoherent student style is "clear enough." It depicts clearly an incoherent mind, an incoherent student. Looked at in this way, all prose is clear. What revision aims for is to "clear up" the student, to present a self more coherent, more in control. A mind thinking, not a mind asleep. It aims, that is, not to denature the human relationship the prose sets up, but to enhance and enrich it. It is not trying to squeeze out the expression of personality but to make such expression possible, not trying to squeeze out all record of a particular occasion and its human relationships but to make them maximally clear. Again, this is why we worry so much about bad prose. It signifies incoherent people, failed social relationships. This worry makes sense only if we feel that prose, ideally, should express human relationships and feelings, not abolish them.

Think, for example, about a familiar piece of prose we might all agree to be successful, Lincoln's Gettysburg Address. Its brevity has been much praised, but the brevity does not work in a vacuum. It makes sense, becomes expressive, only in relation to the occasion. Lincoln took for his subject the inevitable gap between words and deeds. At Gettysburg, this gap was enormous, and the shortness of Lincoln's speech symbolizes just this gap. No speech could do justice to what had happened at Gettysburg. Lincoln's brevity did not *remove* the emotion of the occasion but *intensified* it. It did not ignore the occasion's human relationships but celebrated them. We think of it as a monument to brevity and clarity not because it neutralizes human emotion but because it so superbly enshrines just the emotions which fit that occasion.

We might, as a contrasting example, consider a modern instance of public prose. In 1977, the Federal Aviation Administration published a document called *Draft Environmental Impact Statement for the Proposed Public Acquisition of the Existing Hollywood-Burbank Airport.* It discussed, in two volumes and about fifteen hundred pages, the noise and pollution problems the airport caused and what might happen if the Lockheed Corporation sold it to a consortium of interested city governments. The *Statement* also included extensive testimony about the airport by private citizens. The *Statement* itself provides a perfect — if at times incomprehensible — example of The Official Style; the citizens, with some exceptions, speak and write plain English. The *Statement* as a whole thus constitutes an invaluable extended example of how the two styles conflict in real life.

The issue posed was simple. Lockheed was going to shut the airport down and sell the land if the city governments didn't buy it. Would the loss of airport jobs and public transportation be compensated by the increased peace and quiet in the East San Fernando Valley? Horrible noise on the one hand; money on the other. How do you relate them to one another? The different styles in the *Statement* put the problem in different ways. They seem, sometimes, to be describing different problems. Here's a sample of the *Statement's* archetypal Official Style:

> The findings of ongoing research have shown that a number of physiological effects occur under conditions of noise exposure. . . . These studies demonstrate that noise exposure does influence bodily changes, such as the so-called vegetative functions, by inhibition of gastric juices, lowered skin resistance, modified pulse rate and increased metabolism. . . .
>
> Other studies have investigated the generalized physiological effects of noise in relation to cardiovascular disturbances, gastrointestinal problems, impairment of performance on motor tracking tasks and vascular disturbances, as well as various physical ailments. Miller (1974) states that, "Steady noise of 90 dB increases tension in all muscles." Welch (1972) concludes that "environmental sound has all-pervasive effects on the body, influencing virtually every organ system and function that has been studied," and Cohen (1971) summarized that "the distressing effects

of noise alone or combined with other stress factors can eventually overwhelm man's capability for healthy adjustment with resultant physical or mental ailments." . . .

The VTN survey determined the presence of annoyance reactions which have been identified as indicators of stressful response to environmental noise among respondents both inside and outside the noise impact area. As is reported in Section 2.5.3 (Annoyance Reactions as Determinants of Community Response to Airport Noise) of this chapter, individuals' beliefs about the noise and the noise source tend to determine their reactions to its occurrence and the amount of disturbance it creates. . . .

When asked for the three things they liked least about their neighborhood, 14.2 percent of the respondents in the high noise exposure area, compared to only 5.3 percent of those residing in the low noise exposure area, indicated aircraft noise among the three. It appears from these observations that Hollywood-Burbank Airport does produce annoyance reactions among residents of the East Valley, which indicates a perception of environmental stress associated with Airport noise.

No need to do a detailed analysis at this stage of the game — the formula as before. In this distanced and impersonal world, no one ever suffers; they experience "the presence of annoyance reactions." And, in the report's ever-cautious style, it only "appears" that the airport produces such reactions among residents. Later, in the residents' comments, that "appearance" becomes an oppressive reality.

Human beings, we need to remind ourselves here, are social beings. Our reality is a social reality. Our identity draws its felt life from our relation to other people. We become uneasy if, for extended periods of time, we neither hear nor see other people. We feel uneasy with The Official Style for the same reason. It has no human voice, no face, no personality behind it. It creates no society, encourages no social conversation. We feel that it is *unreal*. The "better" it is, the more typical, the more unreal it becomes. And so we can answer the question of whether you can write a "good" Official Style. No. Not unless you want to erase human reality, make The Official Style yet more Official.

But public prose need not erase human reality. It can do just the opposite, as in the following passage from the same report — a letter from a homeowners' group president. With it, we return to human life.

Our Homeowners Association was formed about a year and a half ago principally because of an overwhelming fear of what might happen to our homes, schools and community as a result of any steps which might be taken by Lockheed and/or the City of Burbank. Our community is inexorably linked to Hollywood-Burbank Airport. The northern part of the North/South runway is in our city. . . .

Our community consists of a vast majority of single-family residences, and long-time owners with "paid in full" or "almost paid up" mortgages. We have been told, "You moved in next to the airport, it was there before you were." This is true in most cases. But, and this is a big "but" — it was an entirely different airport when most of us moved into the area. 20 to 25 years ago, the airport was "home" to small planes. We actually enjoyed watching them buzz around, and many of us spent Sunday afternoons at the airport while our children were amused watching the little planes. However, the advent of the jet plane at HBA changed the entire picture. Suddenly we were the neighbors of a Noise Factory! . . .

Our children are bombarded with noise in 2 local

elementary schools, Roscoe and Glenwood. Teachers have to stop teaching until the noise passes over and everyone waits "for the next one." If the school audiometrist wants an in-depth test for a child with questionable hearing, the child must be taken away from the school altogether to eliminate outside noises.

Our backyards, streets, parks and churches, too, are inundated with noise . . . noise is an ever-constant fact of life for us. There is seldom a time when one cannot hear a plane somewhere in the vicinity — it may be "up" or it may be "down," but once a motor is turned on, we hear it!

We might well be asked, "Why do you continue to live in such a place?" Put in plain and simple terms — we have no place else to go! Years have passed and we have put more money into our mortgages and into our property. We have developed long-time friendships with neighbors and the Community. We don't want to move! . . .

Where do we go? Who is going to pay us — and how much will we be paid — for being uprooted? Who sets the price on losing a street and an entire neighborhood full of long-time friends? If 7 schools are to be closed, where do the children go? What happens to the faculty and staff at the schools? The parochial schools? The small business man who sells consumer goods — what happens when there is no one to sell to?

A living voice! Human society! Plain English, in such a context, takes on the moral grandeur of epic, of the high style. The language of ordinary life reasserts our common humanity. Precisely the humanity, we have now come to see, The Official Style seeks to banish. It is a bad style, then, because it denatures human relations. When we consider that it is becoming the accepted language for the

organizations that govern human relations, we can begin
to see how stylistic and moral issues converge.

Our current Composition Crisis may come, then,
from more than inattention, laziness, or even the diaboli-
cal purposes of The Official Style. It may come, ul-
timately, from our meager ideal for prose. We say that
what we want is only a serviceable tool — useful, neutral,
durable, honest, practical, and so on. But none of us takes
such an attitude even toward our tools! If we earn our
living with them, we love them. We clean and polish
and lubricate them. We prefer one kind to another for
quirky, personal reasons. We modify them. We want them
not only to do a job but to express us, the attitude we take
toward our job. So, too, with prose. We hunger for ceremony, for attitude, for ornament. It is no accident that
bureaucrats play games with buzz words, build what
amounts to purely ornamental patterns. These games
express an attitude, albeit an ironically despairing one,
toward what they are doing, the spirit in which they work.
Jargons are created, too, for the same reason, to express a
mystique, the spirit in which work is conducted. And, like
a student's incoherence, they have their own eloquence,
are clear about a habit of thought, a way of doing business. When we object to the prose, we are really objecting
to the habit of thought, the bureaucratic way of life. It is
because, paradoxically enough, the style is so clear, so successfully communicates a style of life, that we so object to
it.

We have two choices, then, in regard to prose. We can
allow the expression of personality and social relationships and try to control them, or we can ban them and
try to extinguish them. Perhaps we should try the first alternative for a while. We've tried the second for the better
part of a century and we know where it leads. It leads to
where we are now, to The Official Style. For the do-it-
yourselfer who wants to improve his prose, the choice is

even clearer. Even if society disregards the importance of words, you must go in the other direction, train yourself to notice them and to notice them first. A style that at first seems peculiar may not be a "bad" style but simply eloquent about an unexpected kind of reality, one that you may or may not like. Try to keep clear in your mind when you are responding to the words and when to the situation they represent. You'll find that you do first the one and then the other. You'll be rehearsing the same kind of oscillation we have already found to be at the base of stylistic revision. You'll have trained your pattern of attention in just the same way that an artist trains his eyes or a musician his ears. After all, you can't revise what you can't see. Only by learning to see the styles around you can you go beyond a fixed set of rules, a paramedic procedure. In fact, in the long run, that is what any fixed set of rules ideally ought to do. It ought to start you out in training your verbal vision, to show you how to *expand it*. Rules, analytic devices, are a shortcut to vision but no real substitute for it. The paramedic analogy here breaks down. Beyond paramedicine lies medicine; beyond the specific analysis of specific style — what we have been doing here — lies the study of style in general. Verbal style can no more be fully explained by a set of rules, stylistic or moral, than can any other kind of human behavior. Intuition, *trained* intuition, figures as strongly in the one as in the other. You must learn how to see.

Prose style, then, does not finally come down to a set of simple rules about clarity, brevity, and sincerity. It is as complicated as the rest of human behavior and this because it is part of that behavior as well as an expression of it. People who tell you prose style is simple are kidding you. They make reading and writing grotesquely simplistic. They make it unreal. Students often complain about the "unreality" of their school life, but just where it is most real — in the central act of verbal expression — they most yearn for simplification. Well, you can't have it both ways. You can choose the moralizing, rule-centered world, with the simplistic static conception of self and society, but you must not be surprised, when you try to use it in the real world, if it seems "unreal" in theory and backfires in practice. The other road is harder. You have to read and write and pay attention to both. If you do, you'll begin to see with what finesse we can communicate the subtleties of behavior. You'll begin, for the first time, to become self-conscious about the language you speak and hence about the society you live in. You will become more alive. And you'll begin to suspect the real answer to the question, "Why bother?" Because it's fun.

APPENDIX: TERMS

You can see things you don't know the names for but in prose style as in everything else it is easier to see what you know how to describe. The psychological ease that comes from calling things by their proper name has been much neglected in such writing instruction as still takes place. As a result, students usually find themselves reduced to talking about "smoothness," "flow," and other meaningless generalities when they are confronted by a text. And so here are some basic terms.

PARTS OF SPEECH

In traditional English grammar, there are eight parts of speech: verbs, nouns, pronouns, adjectives, adverbs, prepositions, conjunctions, interjections. *Grammar,* in its most general sense, refers to all the rules which govern how meaningful statements can be made in any language. *Syntax* refers to sentence structure, to word order. *Diction* means simply word choice. *Usage* means linguistic custom.

Verbs

1. Verbs have two voices, active and passive:
   An *active verb* indicates the subject acting:
   > Jack *kicks* Bill.
   A *passive verb* indicates the subject acted upon:
   > Bill *is kicked* by Jim.

2. Verbs come in three moods: indicative, subjunctive, and imperative:

A verb in the *indicative mood* says that something is in fact. If it asks a question, it is a question about a fact:
Jim *kicks* Bill. *Has* Jim *kicked* Bill yet?

A verb in the *subjunctive mood* says that something is a wish or thought rather than a fact:
If Jim *were* clever, he *would* trick Bill.

A verb in the *imperative mood* issues a command:
Jim, *kick* Bill!

3. A verb can be either *transitive* or *intransitive.*

A *transitive verb* takes a direct object:
Jim kicks *Bill.*

An *intransitive verb* does not take a direct object. It represents action without a specific goal:
Jim *kicks* with great gusto.

The verb "to be" ("is," "was," etc.) is often called a *linking verb* because it links subject and predicate without transmitting a specific action:
Jim *is* a skunk.

4. English verbs have six tenses: present, past, present perfect, past perfect, future, and future perfect:

Present: Jim *kicks* Bill. (Present progressive: Jim *is kicking* Bill.)
Past: Jim *kicked* Bill.
Present perfect: Jim *has kicked* Bill.
Past perfect: Jim *had kicked* Bill.
Future: Jim *will kick* Bill.
Future perfect: Jim *will have kicked* Bill.

The present perfect, past perfect, and future perfect are called *compound tenses.*

5. Verbs in English have three so-called *infinitive forms: infinitive, participle,* and *gerund.* These verb forms often function as adjectives or nouns.

> *Infinitive: To kick* Jim makes great sport. ("To kick" is here the subject of "makes.")

> Participles and gerunds have the same form; when the form is used as an adjective, it is called a *participle;* when used as a noun, a *gerund.*

> *Participles.* Present participle: Jim is in a truly *kicking* mood. Past participle: Bill was a very well-*kicked* fellow.

> *Gerund: Kicking* Bill is an activity hugely enjoyed by Jim.

(When a word separates the "to" in an infinitive from its complementary form, as in "to directly stimulate" instead of "to stimulate," the infinitive is said to be a *split infinitive.* Most people think this ought not to be done unless absolutely necessary.)

Verbs which take "it" or "there" as subjects are said to be in an *impersonal construction,* e.g., "It has been decided to fire him" or "There has been a personnel readjustment."

Nouns

A noun names something or somebody. A proper noun names a particular being — Jim.
1. Number. The singular number refers to one ("a cat"); plural to more than one ("five cats").
2. Collective nouns. Groups may be thought of as a single unit, as in "the army."

Pronouns

A pronoun is a word used instead of a noun. There are different kinds:
1. Personal pronouns — e.g., I, me, you, he, him, them
2. Intensive pronouns — e.g., myself, yourself, himself

3. Relative pronouns — e.g., who, which, that. These must have *antecedents,* words they refer back to. "Jim has a talent (antecedent) which (relative pronoun) Bill does not possess."
4. Indefinite pronouns — e.g., somebody, anybody, anything
5. Interrogative pronouns — e.g., who?, what?

Possessives

Singular: A worker's hat. Plural: The workers' hats. ("It's," however, equals "it is." The possessive is "its.")

Adjectives

An *adjective* modifies a noun, e.g., "Jim was a *good* hiker."

Adverbs

An *adverb* modifies a verb, e.g., "Jim kicked *swiftly.*"

Prepositions

A *preposition* connects a noun or pronoun with a verb, an adjective, or another pronoun, e.g., "I ran *into* her arms" or "The girl *with* the blue scarf."

Conjunctions

Conjunctions join sentences or parts of them. There are two kinds, coordinating and subordinating.
1. Coordinating conjunctions — e.g., and, but, or, for — connect statements of equal status, e.g., "Bill ran and Jim fell" or "I got up but soon fell down."
2. Subordinating conjunctions — e.g., that, who, when — connect a main clause with a subordinate one, e.g., "I thought *that* he had gone."

Interjection

A sudden outcry, e.g., "Wow!"

SENTENCES

Every sentence must have both a subject and verb, stated or implied, e.g., "Jim (subject) kicks (verb)."

Three kinds

1. A *declarative sentence* states a fact, e.g., "Jim kicks Bill."
2. An *interrogative sentence* asks a question, e.g., "Did Jim kick Bill?"
3. An *exclamatory sentence* registers an exclamation, e.g., "Like, I mean, you know, like wow!"

Three basic structures

1. A *simple sentence* makes one self-standing assertion, i.e., has one main clause, e.g., "Jim kicks Bill."
2. A *compound sentence* makes two or more self-standing assertions, i.e., has two main clauses, e.g., "Jim kicks Bill and Bill feels it" or "Jim kicks Bill and Bill feels it and Bill kicks back."
3. A *complex sentence* makes one self-standing assertion and one or more dependent assertions, subordinate clauses, dependent on the main clause, e.g., "Jim, who has been kicking Bill these twenty-five years, kicks him still and, what's more, still enjoys it."

In *compound sentences,* the clauses are connected by *coordinate conjunctions,* in *complex sentences* by *subordinate clauses.*

Restrictive and nonrestrictive relative clauses

A restrictive clause modifies directly, and so restricts the meaning of the antecedent it refers back to, e.g., "This is the tire *which blew out on the freeway.*" One specific tire is intended. In such clauses the relative clause is *not* set off by a comma.

A nonrestrictive clause, though still a dependent clause, does not directly modify its antecedent and is set off by commas. "These tires, which are quite expensive, last a very long time."

Appositives

An *appositive* is an amplifying word or phrase placed next to the term it refers to and set off by commas, e.g., "Henry VIII, *a glutton for punishment,* had six wives."

BASIC SENTENCE PATTERNS

What words do you use to describe the basic syntactic patterns in a sentence? In addition to the basic types, declarative, interrogative, and exclamatory, and the basic forms of simple, compound, and complex, other terms sometimes come in handy.

Parataxis and Hypotaxis

Parataxis: Phrases or clauses arranged independently, in a coordinate construction, and often without connectives, e.g., "I came, I saw, I conquered."

Hypotaxis: Phrases or clauses arranged in a dependent, subordinate relationship, e.g., "I came, and after I came and looked around a bit, I decided, well, why not, and so conquered."

The adjectival forms are *paratactic* and *hypotactic,* e.g., "Hemingway favors a paratactic syntax while Faulkner prefers a hypotactic one."

Asyndeton and Polysyndeton

Asyndeton: Connectives are omitted between words, phrases, or clauses, e.g., "I've been stressed, destressed, beat down, beat up, held down, held up, conditioned, reconditioned."

Polysyndeton: Connectives are always supplied between words, phrases, or clauses, as when Milton talks about Satan pursuing his way, "And swims, or sinks, or wades, or creeps, or flies."

The adjectives are *asyndetic* and *polysyndetic.*

Periodic Sentence

A periodic sentence is a long sentence with a number of elements, usually balanced or antithetical, standing in a clear syntactical relationship to each other. Usually it suspends the conclusion of the sense until the end of the sentence, and so is sometimes said to use a *suspended syntax.* A perfect example is the passage from Lord

Brougham's defense of Queen Caroline quoted in Chapter 3. A periodic sentence shows us a pattern of thought that has been fully worked out, whose power relationships of subordination have been carefully determined, and whose timing has been climactically ordered. In a periodic sentence, the mind has finished working on the thought, left it fully formed.

There is no equally satisfactory antithetical term for the opposite kind of sentence, a sentence whose elements are loosely related to one another, follow in no particularly antithetical climactic order, and do not suspend its grammatical completion until the close. Such a style is often called a *running style* or a *loose style,* but the terms remain pretty vague. The loose style, we can say, often reflects a mind *in the process of thinking* rather than, as in the periodic sentence, having already completely ordered its thinking. A sentence so loose as to verge on incoherence is often called a *run-on sentence.*

Isocolon

The Greek word means, literally, syntactic units of equal length, and it is used in English to describe the repetition of phrases of equal length and corresponding structure. Preachers, for example, often depend on isocolon to build up a rhythmic pattern or develop a series of contrasting ideas. Falstaff parodies this habit in Shakespeare's *I Henry IV:* "Well, God give *thee the spirit of persuasion* and *him the ears of profiting,* that *what thou speakest may move* and *what he hears may be believed,* that *the true prince* may, for recreation sake, prove *a false thief."* And later in the play, "Harry, now I do *not* speak to thee *in drink but in tears, not in pleasure but in passion, not in words only, but in woes also."*

Chiasmus

Chiasmus is the basic pattern of antithetical inversion, the *AB:BA* pattern. The best example is probably from President John Kennedy's first inaugural address:

$$\text{A} \qquad\qquad \text{B}$$

"Ask not *what your country can do for you,* but

$$\text{B} \qquad\qquad \text{A}$$

what *you can do*   *for your country.*

Anaphora

When you begin a series of phrases, clauses, or sentences with the same word, you are using anaphora. So Churchill during the fall of France in 1940: *"We* have become the sole champion now in arms to defend the world cause. *We shall* do our best to be worthy of this high honor. *We shall* defend our island home, and with the British Empire *we shall* fight on unconquerable until the curse of Hitler is lifted from the brows of mankind. *We* are sure that in the end all will come right."

NOUN STYLE AND VERB STYLE

Every sentence must have a noun and a verb, but one can be emphasized, sometimes almost to the exclusion of the other. The Official Style—strings of prepositional phrases and "is"—exemplifies a noun style *par excellence.* Here are three examples, the first of a noun style, the second of a verb style, and the third of a balanced noun-verb mixture.

1. There is in turn a two-fold structure of this "binding-in." In the first place, by virtue of internalization of the standard, conformity with it tends to be of personal, expressive and/or instrumental significance to ego. In the second place, the structuring of the reactions of alter to ego's action as sanctions is a function of his conformity with the standard. Therefore conformity as a direct mode of the fulfillment of his own need-dispositions tends to coincide with the conformity as a condition of eliciting the favorable and avoiding the unfavorable reactions of others. (Talcott Parsons, *The Social System* [Glencoe, Ill.: Free Press, 1951], p. 38)

2. Patrols, sweeps, missions, search and destroy. It con-

tinued every day as if part of sunlight itself. I went to the colonel's briefings everyday. He explained how effectively we were keeping the enemy off balance, not allowing them to move in, set up mortar sites, and gather for attack. He didn't seem to hate them. They were to him like pests or insects that had to be kept away. It seemed that one important purpose of patrols was just for them to take place, to happen, to exist; there had to be patrols. It gave the men something to do. Find the enemy, make contact, kill, be killed, and return. Trap, block, hold. In the first five days, I lost six corpsmen — two killed, four wounded. (John A. Parrish, *12, 20 & 5: A Doctor's Year in Vietnam* [Baltimore: Penguin Books, 1973], p. 235)

3. We know both too much and too little about Louis XIV ever to succeed in capturing the whole man. In externals, in the mere business of eating, drinking, and dressing, in the outward routine of what he loved to call the *metier du roi,* no historical character, not even Johnson or Pepys, is better known to us; we can even, with the aid of his own writings, penetrate a little of the majestic façade which is *Le Grand Roi.* But when we have done so, we see as in a glass darkly. Hence the extraordinary number and variety of judgments which have been passed upon him; to one school, he is incomparably the ablest ruler in modern European history; to another, a mediocre blunderer, pompous, led by the nose by a succession of generals and civil servants; whilst to a third, he is no great king, but still the finest actor of royalty the world has ever seen. (W. H. Lewis, *The Splendid Century: Life in the France of Louis XIV* [N.Y.: Anchor Books, 1953], p. 1)

PATTERNS OF RHYTHM AND SOUND

Meter

The terms used for scanning (marking the meter of) poetry sometimes prove useful for prose as well.

iamb: unstressed syllable followed by a stressed one, e.g., in·vólve

trochee: opposite of iamb, e.g., ám·bĕr

anapest: two unstressed syllables and one stressed syllable, e.g., thĕre hē góes

dactyl: opposite of anapest, one stressed syllable followed by two unstressed ones, e.g., óp·ēr·āte

These patterns form *feet.* If a line contains two, it is a *dimeter;* three, a *trimeter;* four, a *tetrameter;* five, a *pentameter;* six, a *hexameter.* The adjectival forms are *iambic, trochaic, anapestic,* and *dactylic.*

Sound Resemblances

Alliteration: This originally meant the repetition of initial consonant sounds but came to mean repetition of consonant sounds wherever they occurred, and now is often used to indicate vowel sound repetition as well. You can use it as a general term for this kind of sound play: "Peter Piper picked a peck of pickled peppers"; "Bill will always swill his fill."

Homoioteleuton: This jawbreaker refers, in Latin, to words with similar endings, usually case-endings. An English analogy would be "looked" and booked." You can use it for cases like this, to describe, for example, the "shun" words — "function," "organization," "facilitation" — and the sound clashes they cause.

For further explanation of the basic terms of grammar, see George O. Curme's *English Grammar* in the Barnes & Noble College Outline Series. For a fuller discussion of rhetorical terms like *chiasmus* and *asyndeton,* see Richard A. Lanham's *A Handlist of Rhetorical Terms* in the University of California Press's Campus Paperback Series.